WITTGENSTEIN'S *TRACTATUS*

Wittgenstein once wrote, "The philosopher strives to find the liberating word, that is, the word that finally permits us to grasp what up until now has intangibly weighed down our consciousness." Would Wittgenstein have been willing to describe the *Tractatus* as an attempt to find "the liberating word"? The basic contention of this strikingly innovative new study of the *Tractatus* is that this is precisely the case. Matthew Ostrow argues that, far from seeking to offer a new theory in logic in the tradition of Frege and Russell, Wittgenstein from the very beginning viewed all such endeavors as the ensnarement of thought.

Providing a lucid and systematic analysis of the *Tractatus,* Professor Ostrow argues that Wittgenstein's ultimate aim is to put an end to philosophy itself. The book belongs to a new school of interpretation that sees the early Wittgenstein as denying the possibility of a philosophical theory as such. It is unique, however, in two respects. First, it is the only "nonstandard" reading that offers an extended account of the central topics of the *Tractatus* – the picture theory, the notion of the variable, ethics, the different sense of analysis, and the general form of the proposition. Second, it highlights the intrinsic obstacles to any kind of general or summary understanding of Wittgenstein's thought.

> " . . . an original, detailed and highly compelling interpretation of Wittgenstein's philosophical aims and central concerns. Ostrow shares Diamond's and Conant's sense of dissatisfaction with the traditional readings of the work, but the interpretation he offers is significantly different from theirs and represents the first book-length attempt to develop an alternative approach in a systematic way which engages fully the details of Wittgenstein's text."
>
> – Marie McGinn, University of York

Wittgenstein's *Tractatus*

A Dialectical Interpretation

MATTHEW B. OSTROW

Boston University

CAMBRIDGE
UNIVERSITY PRESS

PUBLISHED BY THE PRESS SYNDICATE OF THE UNIVERSITY OF CAMBRIDGE
The Pitt Building, Trumpington Street, Cambridge, United Kingdom

CAMBRIDGE UNIVERSITY PRESS
The Edinburgh Building, Cambridge CB2 2RU, UK
40 West 20th Street, New York, NY 10011-4211, USA
10 Stamford Road, Oakleigh, VIC 3166, Australia
Ruiz de Alarcón 13, 28014 Madrid, Spain
Dock House, The Waterfront, Cape Town 8001, South Africa

http://www.cambridge.org

First published 2002

Printed in the United States of America

Typeface Meridien 10/13 pt. *System* DeskTopPro/UX [BV]

A catalog record for this book is available from the British Library.

Library of Congress Cataloging in Publication Data
Ostrow, Matthew B., 1961–
Wittgenstein's Tractatus : a dialectical interpretation / Matthew B. Ostrow.
p. cm.
Includes bibliographical references (p.) and index.
ISBN 0-521-80936-3 – ISBN 0-521-00649-X (pb.)
1. Wittgenstein, Ludwig, 1889–1951. Tractatus logico-philosophicus. 2. Logic, Symbolic and mathematical. 3. Language and languages – Philosophy. I. Title.

B3376.W563 T73545 2002
192–dc21 2001035057

ISBN 0 521 80936 3 hardback
ISBN 0 521 00649 X hardback

In memory of my mother

CONTENTS

PREFACE

This book grew out of a larger project, an attempt to draw a philosophical connection between the early Wittgenstein and Plato. While I continue to believe that such a connection exists and that it can be interestingly drawn, the original study, as it stood, was too ambitious; over time, I have come to the (perhaps painfully obvious) realization that a serious attempt to come to terms just with Wittgenstein's *Tractatus* is more than enough for one book. Nonetheless, what initially motivated the project is what, at bottom, continues to draw me to Wittgenstein: the concern with the nature of philosophy itself. Indeed, I believe that for Wittgenstein – early, middle, and late – the question of philosophy's nature is *the* central question of all of philosophy.

Such a contention may seem surprising. For while Wittgenstein's reflections on the philosophical activity, particularly those in the middle of the *Philosophical Investigations,*[1] are among his most oft-quoted claims, we must acknowledge that these represent only a very small portion of his total writings. Moreover, in the *Tractatus,* the text with which we shall chiefly be concerned here, the issue is almost entirely absent, forming the subject matter of a mere eight remarks (TLP 4.111–4.116). In order to view Wittgenstein as placing such primacy on the question of philosophy, it might then seem that we would have to give extraordinary weight to just a few passages.

But this will not be our approach. Instead of seeking to privilege the meager store of Wittgenstein's general reflections on philosophy, we shall take as our starting point the complete set of remarks that make up the *Tractatus.* Such an approach makes it evident that Wittgenstein, as we shall read him, does not understand the question of philosophy's nature to be some "meta-issue," but, rather, one that pervades what one ordinarily would think of as the content of the discipline. The traditional concerns *of* philosophy are, we might say, transformed by Wittgenstein into the means by which we can reflect *on* philosophy. It is the fundamental task of what follows to seek to bring out how this can be the case.

Many people have helped me, in one way or another, with the lengthy process of writing this book. First and foremost, I would like to thank the late Burton Dreben. I am thankful to him as a teacher: He showed me what it is to think about philosophy at the highest level. I am thankful to him as the keenest of critics and collaborators: He spent many hours with me working through the nuances of my reading of the *Tractatus*. And I am thankful to him as a friend: His kindness, humor, and interest in my work were invaluable to me. Nearly every page of this study reflects his powerful influence and I remain deeply indebted to him.

Charles Griswold also played a central role in the birth and development of this book. His subtle and imaginative reading of the Platonic dialogues provided part of the spark for the initial project. Furthermore, I am deeply grateful to him for his ongoing support, advice, and encouragement.

Juliet Floyd was exceedingly generous with her help and encouragement in nearly every phase of the writing process. Moreover, I have been very much influenced by her penetrating and original reading of Wittgenstein, and by exposure to the elegance of her philosophical style. I owe her a large debt of gratitude.

I would also like to thank Terence Moore and Matthew Lord of Cambridge University Press and my Production Editor, Laura Lawrie, for their assistance and support. I am grateful as well to the Earhart Foundation for the two years of financial support during the study that formed the indispensable background to this book.

Many others have contributed to this study – perhaps at times without even realizing it – and indeed deserve greater acknowledgment than I can offer here. I have had extensive and very fruitful conversations about the *Tractatus* with Rosalind Carey, Denis McManus, Joe McDonald, Andrew Lugg, and Anat Biletzki, and about philosophy more generally with Bruce Fraser, Thomas Woodard, Lawrence Pasternack, Phil Cafaro, Klaus Brinkmann, David Roochnik, and my brothers, Michael and Daniel Ostrow. Victor Kestenbaum took an interest in my work and offered his advice and encouragement at a time when these were sorely needed. David Stern provided very helpful comments on an earlier draft.

I have also had enumerable philosophical conversations with my wife, Theresa Reed. For that alone she would deserve my ample thanks, but, happily, her involvement with this study has extended far beyond that capacity, far beyond, in truth, what I can begin to express. Suffice it to say that this book would in no way have been possible without her.

Finally, I would like to thank my father, Seymour Ostrow, and my late mother, Judith Alling, who I dearly wish were still here to discuss it with me.

INTRODUCTION

I

Wittgenstein, in conversation with Moritz Schlick, once characterized his fundamental goal in philosophy as follows: "Everything we do consists in trying to find the liberating word (*erloesende Wort*)" (VC 77). Similarly, we find in The Big Typescript: "The philosopher strives to find the liberating word, that is, the word that finally permits us to grasp what up until now has intangibly weighed down our consciousness" (PO 165).[1] Both remarks were made in the 1930s, years after the publication of the *Tractatus:* with their depiction of philosophy as the pathway out of psychic encumbrance, they quite naturally call to mind Wittgenstein's later, explicitly "therapeutic" thought (cf., e.g., PI 133). But, we might ask, could such claims be applied to Wittgenstein's early work as well? Would Wittgenstein have been willing to describe the *Tractatus* itself as an effort to find "the liberating word"? My fundamental contention in this book is that this is indeed the case, that, far from seeking to offer a new theory of logic, to continue the philosophical legacies of Frege and Russell, Wittgenstein from the start views all such endeavors as the ensnarement of thought. The *Tractatus,* I shall aim to show, is nothing but an attempt to set down in definitive fashion the way of release.

For those involved in writing and reflecting on early analytic philosophy, such an assertion is likely at once to locate this study in the grid of a familiar set of dichotomies. It would seem to herald a non-metaphysical interpretation of the *Tractatus* as opposed to a standard, metaphysical reading, an emphasis on the continuity of Wittgenstein's thought rather than the notion of a radical break from an earlier, more traditional philosophical stance, an insistence on the nonsensicality of the text's propositions as against the possibility that they might manage to communicate a kind of indirect truth.[2] And, in a very broad sense, those expectations will be met by what follows. But what animates this book is the belief that that "sense" is entirely *too* broad – that is, that the terms in which these standard oppositions are formulated are simply not adequate to the *Tractatus.* Do we really know in general just what it means for a proposition or set of propositions to be "metaphysical" rather than "nonmetaphysical"? Is the fundamental aim of a philosopher's thought so open to view that we can at once recognize when a given piece of writing does or does not cohere with it? Do we understand the claim that a work of philosophy is simply "nonsense"? It is not, of course, that Wittgenstein leaves us completely unequipped for such questions; on the contrary, I would suggest that, in one form or another, they lie at the heart of the *Tractatus.* But just this fact renders notions like "metaphysical," "nonsense," and so forth ill-suited to any sort of explanatory task in this context. They are, we might say, too much part of the problem to constitute a potential solution.

One might then imagine that what will here be proposed is an alternative vocabulary in terms of which our interpretation is to be conducted – our own set of privileged categories. But I shall argue shortly against any such strategy. Instead, what we must acknowledge at the start is just the *problem* that is posed by the attempt to interpret the *Tractatus.* If we grant that Wittgenstein's aim here is, in one way or another, to call into question the traditional language of philosophy, we must realize that this is not just the language of Frege, Russell, Moore, et al., but also *our* language: precisely the depth and comprehensiveness of this text's critique of philosophy deprives us of our, as it were, clinical distance as commentators on the text. What we find, I believe inevitably, is that we cannot insulate ourselves from the difficulties with which Wittgenstein is concerned, that the philosophical commitments that are revealed in our own manner of textual analysis are the very subject matter of the *Tractatus.* The *Tractatus* seeks to expose the extraordinary confusions inherent in the process of philosophical inquiry. To understand and write about that text, we must be willing to allow that these might be our confusions as well.

II

In order to get a preliminary view of the difficulties that we must confront, let us then return to the remark with which we began. What does it really mean to read the *Tractatus* in terms of a fundamental concern to "liberate" us from philosophical confusion? One might well grant something of this sort as the young Wittgenstein's aim; he does, after all, already in the Preface portray his book as intending to show that "the problems of philosophy" rest on "the misunderstanding of the logic of our language" (TLP, p. 27).[3] Nonetheless, one could quite naturally construe the basic form of the Tractarian critique, if not its details, in traditional philosophical terms, as an attempt to provide a *refutation* of the misunderstandings and errors of the past. On this reading, Wittgenstein proclaims various philosophical positions to be "nonsense" (see, e.g., TLP 4.003, 5.5351, 6.51) in the way that so many philosophers in the Western tradition have dismissed their predecessors' claims – namely, as being patently false or absurd. Such a view has in fact been implicit in much of the literature on the *Tractatus,* beginning with Ramsey's review[4] and the responses of the Vienna positivists, and continuing with the work of more contemporary commentators like Black,[5] Stenius,[6] Hintikka,[7] Hacker,[8] and Pears.[9] Characteristic of this approach – which would include a quite diverse set of interpretations – is the insistence on treating the Wittgensteinian attack as if it presented, in opposition to the tradition, a series of straightforward philosophical accounts: accounts of the proposition (the "picture theory"), the tautologous nature of logical truth, the ineffability of logical form, and so forth. These accounts are then criticized or modified by commentators in accordance with the demands that are presumably to be satisfied by a well-constructed philosophical theory.

One rather large obstacle to this approach to the *Tractatus* is represented by remark 6.54. Here Wittgenstein famously declares: "My propositions are elucidatory in this way: he who understands me finally recognizes them as nonsensical (*unsinnig*), when he has climbed out through them, on them, over them." If we take this remark seriously, it would appear difficult to treat its author as someone who has intended to present a straightforward theory, a series of claims to be evaluated in terms of their truth value. Still, the responses on the part of Tractarian commentators to this move have been varied. Perhaps most commonly the tendency has been to disregard this remark, or to ignore its consequences with respect to our understanding of the seemingly substantive details of the text. For such readers, this remark is regarded as striking, but not as a central feature to be accommodated within a satisfactory interpretation.[10]

A second type of response involves an attempt at softening the impact of the text's harsh self-assessment. One notable example of the latter strategy is Carnap's interpretation of the statements of the *Tractatus* as purely linguistic proposals.[11] For Carnap, while philosophical propositions of the sort espoused by Wittgenstein (and the Vienna positivists) make no claims about the world and thus are not true or false, they are not like many traditional metaphysical assertions in being entirely nonsensical. Instead, legitimate philosophy is to be understood as consisting of elucidations, purely formal assertions that serve to clarify the logical syntax of the language of science. In this sense, they can be seen as having the empty character that Wittgenstein ascribes to the tautologous propositions of logic.[12]

A second example of an explicit attempt at moderating the *Tractatus'* view of its own utterances is found in commentators like Anscombe,[13] Geach,[14] Hintikka,[15] and Hacker.[16] The strategy they employ is motivated by remarks such as TLP 5.62 ("In fact, what solipsism *means* is quite correct, only it cannot be said, but shows itself."), 4.115 ("[Philosophy] will mean the unspeakable by clearly displaying the speakable.") and 4.1211 ("Thus a proposition 'f*a*' shows that in its sense the object *a* occurs, two propositions 'f*a*' and 'g*a*' that they are both about the same object."). In these remarks and elsewhere, Wittgenstein seems to suggest that, while the attempt to state what is properly to be *shown* results in what he calls "nonsense," something intelligible is nonetheless thereby expressed. We are then led to suppose that Wittgenstein's propositions – if not the propositions of all metaphysics – are nonsense only in a special sense. To be sure, so such commentators continue, they are not strictly utterable, according to the standards of significance established by the *Tractatus*. Still, they somehow manage to convey to us important philosophical truths: at the end of the book we "know" that, in reality, the world is composed of facts, not things, that a common logical form binds together language and the world, that value lies outside of the world, and so on. Except, of course, we cannot actually *say* these things, but must only *think* them, silently to ourselves; or perhaps we may repeat them –

grudgingly – to another, but always with the acknowledgment that in so doing we have transgressed the strictly *proper* bounds of sense.

More recently, Cora Diamond, beginning with her important paper "Throwing Away the Ladder," has presented a central challenge to this reading – and, indirectly, to the related interpretation offered by Carnap.[17] Diamond, in effect, attributes to Wittgenstein the position of Ramsey in his oft-quoted *criticism* of the *Tractatus'* notion of showing: "But what we can't say, we can't say and we can't whistle it either."[18] That is, refusing to countenance the possibility of any sort of meaningful gesture toward the ineffable, she bites the bullet on Wittgenstein's behalf and proclaims that, as far as the *Tractatus* is concerned, its own statements really are nonsense, plain and simple. There is no Tractarian counterpart to the Kantian *Ding an sich,* no deep features of reality that are somehow made manifest in Wittgenstein's utterances. Instead, we must take Wittgenstein at his word at 6.54 and realize that, in the end, all the pronouncements of his text are just so much gibberish.

Now I have a good deal of sympathy with – and have been much influenced by – Diamond's approach, and the elaboration of it provided by James Conant. Nonetheless, I think one must take care to be as clear as possible about what this position really comes to, as it can easily serve to mislead. Given the importance of the Conant/Diamond interpretation in framing the contemporary debate about the *Tractatus,* I want then to consider it in some detail (my focus will be on Diamond's initial paper).

To begin with, Diamond suggests that Wittgenstein's conception of nonsense and his concomitant show/say distinction have their roots in Frege's so-called concept "horse" problem. Frege, in the article "Concept and Object," dismisses as incoherent Benno Kerry's contention that there can be concepts – like the concept "horse" – which also can function as objects. For Frege, the concept/object distinction is mutually exclusive: a concept by its very nature is predicative or, as he also puts it, "unsaturated"; conversely, the object, as a logical subject, serves necessarily to fill the gap left by the concept. In Kerry's example, then – "the concept 'horse' is a concept easily attained" – the first three words do not designate a Fregean concept, but, as is indicated by the appearance there of the definite article, a Fregean object. The peculiarity of having to maintain that the concept "horse" is not a concept is dismissed by Frege as an "awkwardness of language" (CP 185) and, moreover, as Diamond reads him, one he believes will not be encountered in a logically perfect notation like his Begriffsschrift. Thus, in the Begriffsschrift, statements about concepts and objects of the sort represented by Kerry's example – indeed, the very claim that there *is* a fundamental distinction between concepts (or functions) and objects – will not be formulatable. Instead, *that* there is such a division will come out in the distinctive use of the signs of the notation.

Diamond then terms remarks like the one expressing the difference between concepts and objects "transitional";[19] their purpose is solely to lead us *into* the Begriffsschrift, to begin operating within its parameters. But once we have effected this transition, these remarks are recognized as completely without sense and are in fact inexpressible. Here we begin to see how Diamond draws the connection with Wittgenstein. For her, Wittgenstein is fundamentally concerned to extend to the whole philosophical vocabulary Frege's way of excluding notions like "function" and "concept." Toward that end, he is understood as having formulated a number of transitional statements – namely remarks 1–6.522 of the *Tractatus. All* these claims, as transitional, will then have to be given up by the close of the *Tractatus.* After we have read – and understood – the text, we cannot suppose ourselves to be left hinting at some important truth with a statement like "The world is the totality of facts, not things," any more than we would suppose this about an attempt to state something about functions and objects from within the Begriffsschrift. Instead, 1.1, like every other remark of the *Tractatus,* is now seen as it really is – that is, as a claim completely on par with "Socrates is frabble"[20] or " 'Twas brillig, and the slithy toves did gyre and gimble in the wabe."[21] To attempt to ascribe any further content to Wittgenstein's claims is, for her, to "chicken out."

A quite natural first response to this approach focuses on the extraordinary expressive power it attributes to the supposed gibberish of the *Tractatus.* For clearly it is not at once obvious that this text's propositions are utter nonsense, any more than it is obvious that the traditional claims of metaphysics have such a character. If it were obvious, if the *Tractatus,* Russell's *Principles of Mathematics,* Aristotle's *Metaphysics,* and so forth were plainly indistinguishable from Lewis Carroll's "Jabberwocky," none of these works could ever have the power to mislead. (Why haven't any books been written claiming to have established the nonsensicality of the Carroll poem?) Wittgenstein's claims are then assumed to be capable of *themselves* effecting the "transition" Diamond describes, of somehow *bringing us* to recognize the fact that they are, contrary to all appearances, absolutely devoid of sense. Indeed, in "What Nonsense Might Be,"[22] Diamond sketches in some detail Wittgenstein's account of the precise *way* in which philosophical nonsense is to be viewed, suggesting, in particular, that he rejects (what Diamond takes to be) Carnap's view that it consists of category errors.[23] But this is as much as to acknowledge the special character of the Tractarian propositions, their dissimilarity to pseudo-sentences like "Socrates is frabble."[24] The latter expression, after all, would seem to have none of the capacity for self-illumination that is thought to belong to the remarks of the *Tractatus.* We might say that it "shows us" that it does not make sense, but this is a result of our understanding the syntax of the English language; if we did not already know that syntax and were not therefore at once inclined to call the expression "meaningless," it surely could not itself *teach* us that (let alone why) this is the case. The point, in short, is that the more that Witttgenstein's claims are assimilated to ordinary nonsense sentences, the less easy it becomes to explain the possibility of our ever coming to recognize them as such.

Diamond, however, might seem to have developed a response to this sort of objection, one which she elaborates in a more recent article, "Ethics, Imagination, and the Method of Wittgenstein's *Tractatus.*"[25] Central to this part of her account is Wittgenstein's emphasis in 6.54 on himself as subject. For, she points out, this remark does not proclaim that he who understands my *propositions* "finally recognizes them as nonsensical," but rather that he who understands *me* so recognizes them.[26] This distinction between understanding the utterer of nonsense and understanding the nonsense itself is, for Diamond, crucial. For while the *Tractatus'* remarks, as devoid of sense, are incapable of being understood in themselves, we can still attempt to understand a *person* who would wish to proclaim such empty strings. This involves "a kind of imaginative activity, an exercise of the capacity to enter into the taking of nonsense for sense, of the capacity to share imaginatively the inclination to think that one is thinking something in it."[27] On this reading, the *Tractatus* is then seen as an attempt to, as it were, conjure up the state of mind of someone who has an inclination toward metaphysics. It does this, however, always with a therapeutic intent – that is, with the aim of helping the individual explode the illusion that fosters his metaphysical tendency. Diamond in this way believes she can account for the illuminating potential of the Tractarian remarks, locating this not in those remarks' "internal features," but rather in external features of their use;[28] what allows Wittgenstein's nonsensical utterances to be liberating is just their utterer's recognition of them *as* nonsense.

But while this account is suggestive and interesting, one still worries about its tendency to inflate the *Tractatus'* notion of nonsense, even while insisting on its ordinariness. What is it about Wittgenstein's supposed babbling that could so stimulate our imaginations, and direct them in such a particular manner? Or, alternatively, one might wonder whether we can really make sense of Diamond's notion of the "imagination" (a term, after all, that does not play much of a role in the *Tractatus*). One wonders how imagination could bring us to "understand" a person, if all we have at our disposal are his absolutely unintelligible strings of words.[29]

How would Diamond reply to these objections? I suspect she would view them as placing a kind of pressure on her interpretation that it was not intended to bear: we could be seen here as fastening on to what is for her only a kind of rhetorical move in a polemic against a confused reading of the *Tractatus*. In other words, her assimilation of metaphysical claims to "plain nonsense" is a means of denying the coherence of the notion of an ineffable content, but should not be viewed as saying anything *more* than that; Diamond's aim is not to provide a genuine characterization of Wittgenstein's remarks. To demand from her an explanation of precisely how the plain nonsense of the *Tractatus* is illuminating could thus be said to miss the point: rather than seeking to provide an account of the mechanism of the text, Diamond's purpose is simply to steer us away from supposing any role for its propositions – *after* that "mechanism" has (somehow) performed its function.

We now can begin to see the real question that is opened up by Diamond's work, especially "Throwing Away the Ladder" and its central idea of the *Tractatus* as a series of "transitional remarks." That question can be brought into full view by here asking ourselves: transitional to *what?* I certainly agree with Cora Diamond's premise that much of the original motivation for both the show/say distinction and the idea of "throwing away the ladder" comes from Frege's concept "horse" problem (as well as the related difficulty inherent in Russell's theory of types). But it would seem to be of paramount importance at this point not to push the parallel too far, to realize that Wittgenstein is shifting quite fundamentally the Fregean perspective. For let us grant for the moment that Frege has a full awareness of the implications of the idea of extra-Begriffsschrift "elucidations." Still, it must be acknowledged that there exists for him a concrete means of avoiding the utterance of such statements – namely, by always working within the confines of his formal language. In other words, Frege's (supposed) contention that certain prose judgments (the "elucidations") can ultimately be transcended gains its force from the fact that one can operate perfectly well with his Begriffsschrift without ever making such judgments. So, for example, a statement like "There are functions and objects" cannot even be formulated within his "concept script" – "$\exists f$ & $\exists x$" is not a well-formed formula – but the language nonetheless allows us to *use* these notions in the formalization of logical inferences. But what is the domain in which Wittgenstein would have us operate, once we have dispensed with the elucidations that constitute the *Tractatus?* There is, of course, a long tradition of Tractarian interpretation, going back to Russell's Introduction to the book (TLP, p. 8), which views Wittgenstein as concerned with laying down conditions for an ideal language. But, while it is unquestionable that the notion of a canonical Begriffsschrift plays an important (if extremely unclear) role in the *Tractatus*, it is equally certain that Wittgenstein has not actually *provided* us with any such language. We cannot confuse what are, at best, indications of some of the elements of a proposed formalism – such as, for example, the absence of a sign for identity – with Frege's systematic specifications in the *Begriffsschrift* and the *Grundgesetze*. The point, then, is that despite Wittgenstein's talk of employing a symbolism that "excludes" the "errors" of traditional philosophy (see TLP 3.325), at the end of the *Tractatus* we remain very much within the context of our "ordinary" language, the same language in which the nonsensical propositions of metaphysics were originally formulated.[30]

The whole idea of an adequate notation can therefore only be part of Wittgenstein's way of leading us to a new *perspective* on logic, as opposed to the adoption of an actual new language. One might then describe the central problem that Diamond and Conant's work points us toward as one of becoming clear on the nature of this perspective, once we understand that it is not embodied, as it were, in a formal language, in a specifiable *method* for eliminating the metaphysical pseudo-sentences. How are we to characterize what the *Tractatus* brings us, in the end, to see? Given the difficulties that we saw above in the attempt to describe that insight in terms of the *literal* unintelligibility of the language of metaphysics, it may be tempting at this point to reach for a notion of "deep nonsense." The propositions of the *Tractatus* really are nonsense, one will now maintain, except not in the plain, garden variety sense. They violate not ordinary syntax, but a deeper underlying structure – what the text refers to as *logical* syntax (see TLP 3.325, 3.33, 3.334, 6.124). We can then hold that it is just toward the recognition of the claims of all metaphysics as nonsense in this special sense that the text aims to bring us.

But this strategy is less promising than it may initially seem, as the appearance of the term "logical syntax" in the above purported exposition of the text's central purpose should indicate. For the necessity of here bringing in the notions of the *Tractatus* itself – the very notions we have presumably "thrown away" at the book's close – indicates the hollowness of supposing that we have, as yet, proffered any sort of explanation. Indeed, one now begins to wonder about the coherence of even *asking* for an explanation in this context. The problem now appears to lie not merely with how to characterize the text's point – whether to describe it as the exposing of deep nonsense or plain nonsense – but with the very notion that we might "characterize" that point at all. The difficulty, we could say, is that we are from the start assuming that the statements proclaiming the nonsensicality of the *Tractatus'* remarks could be *true*. What we are beginning to see, however, is that perhaps Wittgenstein is concerned precisely to deny the possibility of such a neutral assessment of the nature of the text's propositions, of the nature of metaphysical claims generally. What we are beginning to see is that, for Wittgenstein, a sentence like " 'The world is everything that is the case' is nonsense" is *itself* nonsense.

This may seem to leave the would-be reader of the *Tractatus* in a difficult, if not impossible, position. To some, the above claim will appear as a kind of *reductio ad absurdum* of the whole attempt to read this text.[31] Still, while I by no means wish to downplay the peculiarity of the position in which we find ourselves, I would urge that the situation is perhaps not quite so dire. Let us then consider these three sentences:

1. " 'The world is everything that is the case' is nonsense" is nonsense.
2. "The world is everything that is the case" is nonsense.
3. The world is everything that is the case.

The appearance of paradox in (1) would seem to stem from the assumption that the terms that compose this sentence are all used in their ordinary senses – as if we were here committed to asserting the "plain nonsensicality" of the attempt to say anything whatsoever about Wittgenstein's remarks. It is important, however, to emphasize that the term "nonsense" must be interpreted in the same sense in its second occurrence in (1) as in its first occurrence within that sentence (i.e., as it occurs in (2)). That is, we understand what it means to ascribe this property to attempts to characterize statements of the *Tractatus* only to the extent that we understand the meaning of the predicate in the text itself. But to deny, as we have, the possibility of a general characterization of the text's propositions is just to call into question the possibility of making straightforward assertions about "the meaning" of this predicate in the *Tractatus;* it is to claim that an understanding of the term "nonsense" can only be attained through viewing in what Wittgenstein would regard as the appropriate way the (Tractarian) sentences to which it is appended. Precisely *this* point is then expressed by (1): this sentence serves to reflect the reducibility *within* the *Tractatus* of (2) to (3). The sentence (1) is therefore not itself to be construed as somehow paradoxical, but rather as a meaningful and – I would claim – in fact true statement about Wittgenstein's use of the string "nonsense."

At the same time, however, we must recognize the very limited nature of this claim; we must recognize how our capacity to make accurate statements about the *Tractatus* comes at the price of a restriction on their informativeness. For while the above description of the role of certain signs in this text may be correct, this description as yet tells us nothing about what those signs mean – precisely what any commentary on the text is presumably concerned to elucidate. In an interesting way, then, the Fregean concept "horse" dilemma can be seen to extend not only to the *Tractatus* but also to any interpretation of the *Tractatus:* the *commentator* now finds himself in the position of, like Frege, ultimately having to ask for "a pinch of salt"; *he* must appeal to his reader to, as it were, jump into Wittgenstein's text, to begin *using* its language. But this, then, is as much as to admit that our central question about what the *Tractatus* brings us to see can permit no answer. Or, better, it is to admit that whatever is proposed as an answer cannot take the form that one will almost instinctively require of it. For while we can offer restatements, in putatively clearer terms, of what we will claim to be Wittgenstein's point, the force of these considerations is to deprive such restatements of any privileged status, to lead us to see that they must stand on the same level as the propositions of the *Tractatus* itself.

It is now possible to describe in a new way Wittgenstein's declaration of the nonsensicality of his own propositions at 6.54. Rather than a neutral summing-up of the real purpose of the *Tractatus,* this remark would seem to function as a way of orienting us toward the text as a whole, of indicating how we are to read it. Nonsense, we might say, forms the lens through which all Wittgenstein's propositions are to be viewed: we grasp his point just when we are inclined to understand these remarks *as* nonsense. That, of course, is not to explain the meaning of the term "nonsense" in the *Tractatus,* but to face us back toward the text. It is to suggest that the nonsensicality of Wittgenstein's propositions only emerges through a detailed consideration of those propositions themselves, that it cannot be understood apart from such a consideration.[32] My contention, in other words, is that the Wittgensteinian view of the nature of his own claims, of philosophy generally, is not expressible in some self-standing formula, but is rather given entirely in and through the recognition of an intrinsic instability in a particular kind of utterance; it is contained in the seeing *how* our philosophical assertions change their character, *how* they undermine their own initial presentation as straightforward truth claims.[33]

In different terms, what this discussion helps to make evident is the fundamentally *dialectical* nature of Wittgenstein's thought in the *Tractatus.*[34] It brings to the fore the extent to which we are, at every juncture of the book, engaged with the very metaphysics that is apparently being disparaged. Indeed, this dialectic can already be seen at the very beginning of the Preface, where Wittgenstein writes: "This book will perhaps only be understood by those who have themselves already thought the thoughts (*die Gedanken*) which are expressed in it – or similar thoughts" (TLP, p. 27). The appearance here of the metaphysically loaded, Fregean term *Gedanke* signals Wittgenstein's intent. He is not suggesting, as it may initially seem, that only someone who has reached the same "conclusions" as he will be able to understand the book. Rather, the point is that these utterances have no purpose except for one who is genuinely tempted by the *metaphysics* it aims to explode; Wittgenstein's "elucidations" depend for their effect on a prior yearning for the deepest – and therefore, we may come to say, most empty – philosophical *Gedanken*.

This same point is even more evident at the close of the *Tractatus*. At 6.53, Wittgenstein describes the "only strictly correct method" of doing philosophy as an enterprise in which one would say "nothing except what can be said, i.e. the propositions of natural science, i.e., something that has nothing to with philosophy; and then always, when someone else wished to say something metaphysical, [one would] demonstrate to him that he had given no meaning to certain signs in his propositions." In the strict method, in contrast to the method of the *Tractatus*, the metaphysical inclination of Wittgenstein's interlocutor is open to view. Wittgenstein will then be clearly understood as *responding* to a particular kind of utterance, rather than being himself gripped by an urge to spell out a series of novel philosophical claims. But this does not mean that Wittgenstein's claims in this context are now to be regarded as obviously sensical, that his "demonstration" to his interlocutor will be of a fundamentally different nature than the "arguments" of the *Tractatus*. What is regarded by him as "philosophy" will thus again necessarily involve the dialectical engagement with metaphysics, with the urge to transcend the bounds of sense. And that is to say once more that, insofar as we are engaged in this process (what he at 4.112 calls "an activity," as opposed to "a theory"), we are deprived of a neutral standpoint from which to assess its ultimate nature.

III

With the above in mind, we can begin to get a clearer sense of the nature of the "liberation" I have claimed the *Tractatus* aims to bring about. Given the emphasis of so much recent literature on 6.54, one might well suppose that this remark was in fact the text's final statement, that Wittgenstein leaves us with his pronouncement of the nonsensicality of everything philosophical. In fact, though, the *Tractatus* ends with proposition 7's call for silence: "Whereof one cannot speak, thereof one must be silent." Wittgenstein's claims, it would seem, find their real fulfillment not in what we say, but in what we *do*. But this is precisely what is required by the text's stance, as we have characterized it. Wittgenstein's final remark brings out how we are in the end violating the spirit of the text every bit as much by proclaiming the complete and utter nonsensicality of metaphysics, as by proclaiming, for example, that the number 1 is, really is, an *object*. It makes clear that the charge of "nonsense" against philosophy is not a claim alongside the claims of science but another move in the Wittgensteinian dialectic. That is not to deny that the move is one of particular importance. But if that dialectic's purpose is to be achieved, if it is to lead us to "see the world rightly" (TLP 6.54), it must ultimately culminate in its own *cessation*. Liberation, for Wittgenstein, is nothing other than the end of philosophy.

It might then seem that we would best make the *Tractatus'* point by stopping our commentary right here. Of course, Wittgenstein's own continued preoccupation with the problems of philosophy indicates how difficult it can be simply to remain silent. But it is not merely psychological compulsion that might lead us to continue – or, more important, that led Wittgenstein himself to go on with philosophy. For assuming that our aim really was to cease speaking metaphysics, what is it exactly that we are not to say? Consider my own earlier references to Wittgenstein's desire to preclude a "particular kind of utterance."[35] What *kind* of utterance, then? We, of course, want to say "philosophical" or "metaphysical" – but do we really know in advance the extension of those concepts? We are faced here with the essential difficulty of Wittgenstein's dialectical enterprise, the dilemma inherent in the attempt to "draw a limit . . . to the *expression* of thoughts" (TLP, p. 27, emphasis mine). That is: we do not know beforehand exactly what is to count as an illicit, metaphysical claim; we in fact *cannot* know this, since to do so would be to think what the *Tractatus* aims to reveal as not really thinkable.[36]

We could say, then, that the central task of the *Tractatus* is one of somehow delineating the class of those utterances it seeks to eviscerate. For the young Wittgenstein this aim is achieved by becoming clear on what he takes to be these utterances' *essence* – the fundamental impulse that leads us to make them, the single question that he imagines to lie at their heart. Just this view of a unitary core to the problems of philosophy is expressed in Wittgenstein's audacious Preface claim to have found "on all essential points, the[ir] final solution" (TLP, p. 29). The same idea also appears in the *Notebooks,* in which Wittgenstein twice speaks of the sense that his seemingly multifarious investigations are all manifestations of a "single great problem" (see NB 23 and 40). The *Tractatus* is then really nothing but Wittgenstein's extended attempt to characterize that single great problem, the root of the drive toward metaphysics; it is a search for *the* liberating word.

Now this whole line of thought may sound suspiciously reminiscent of the uncharitable reading of Cora Diamond's notion of transitional remarks – as if I were suggesting that Wittgenstein's remarks first make some sort of sense and then subsequently become nonsensical. But my claim is that, for Wittgenstein, the revealing of the essence of metaphysics and the "demonstration" of the nonsensicality of metaphysics are, in fact, two sides of the same coin. To read the *Tractatus* dialectically, in my sense of the term, is to recognize that the successful characterization of philosophy *is* its dismissal as *Unsinn.* Wittgenstein's enterprise is an attempt to lead us to a view of metaphysics so complete that it dissolves itself.

IV

This conception of the aim of the *Tractatus* both clarifies and complicates the task of its would-be interpreter. It is clarified, I believe, in that we now see that we need not tie ourselves up in knots over the question of how the text's nonsense can be illuminating, or of how we can purport to explain what Wittgenstein holds can only be shown. We recognize instead that "nonsense," "show," "explain," like the rest of the terms of the *Tractatus,* have their life only *within* the text, that to seek to make general, philosophically neutral claims about these notions is to mislead (ourselves, as well as others). Our task as commentators is then precisely one of describing, as accurately as possible, the role of those terms; one might say that we are engaged in an act of translation rather than one of explanation. But that is to say that the Tractarian commentator's task is and must be enormously complicated: the successful interpretation will have the same "logical multiplicity" (to borrow a phrase from the *Tractatus*) as what it expounds; it must be as complex and multifarious as the text itself. In the *Philosophical Remarks,* Wittgenstein writes: "Philosophy unties the knots in our thinking, which we have tangled up in an absurd way; but to do that, it must make movements that are just as complicated as the knots. Although the *result* of philosophy is simple, its methods for arriving there cannot be so" (PR 2). This remark holds for the task of Wittgenstein's would-be expositor as well. There is no shortcut, no simplifying, general principles that we can invoke in order to understand the *Tractatus* – only the arduous task of working our way through its many intricate details.

In what follows, we shall involve ourselves in just such a close textual analysis. Chapter I will discuss the opening, "ontological" remarks (TLP 1–2.063) and their connection to the first part of the picture theory (TLP 2.1–2.172). Chapter II will focus on the notion of analysis, as it is presented in the 3s and early 4s. Chapter III will inquire into Wittgenstein's understanding of logical inference, his specific response to the logic of Russell's *Principia Mathematica* and Frege's *Begriffsschrift* and *Grundgesetze*. Here we shall focus on the last part of the picture theory (TLP 2.174–2.225), the discussion of "sense" in the 4s and 5s, and, finally, the *Tractatus'* fundamental notion of the "general form of the proposition."

Our approach to the *Tractatus* will aim to reflect as far as possible its author's view of the unified nature of the inquiry that it represents. Thus, it seeks to be comprehensive, to address, at least to some extent, all the main "topics" with which this text is typically taken to be concerned. In the interest of readability, however, this study falls somewhat short of this ideal: in particular we shall have to ignore or give short shrift to the *Tractatus'* discussions of number, probability, scientific theory, the propositional attitudes, and of solipsism. In the first three cases, we can hope to justify the omissions by attempting to convey (what I would claim is) the chief import of these discussions through our account of the Tractarian notion of the sense of a proposition. And while I would hold that the key ideas motivating Wittgenstein's way of handling the propositional attitudes and solipsism will at least be *familiar* by the end of our study, the importance generally accorded to these notions would demand that, ideally, they be given independent treatment.

There is another important issue that has been conspicuously absent from our discussion thus far. In our focus on questions concerning the logic of the *Tractatus*, we have ignored what Wittgenstein declares, in a famous letter to von Ficker, to be the text's real purpose

– namely, the expression of an "ethical" point.[37] Indeed, just such a dimension is implied by our suggestion that the *Tractatus* is essentially an attempt to "liberate" us from a particular sort of confusion: the word *erloesend,* like its English counterpart, has an explicitly ethical or religious connotation, carrying the sense of something that saves or redeems us; Wittgenstein himself uses a cognate of this word in connection with a discussion of the meaning of Christ's Resurrection.[38] One cannot but then wonder what place this sort of concern could occupy in the text as we have presented it thus far. There are, of course, the relatively small number of remarks toward the end of the *Tractatus* that explicitly address religious-sounding themes. But I believe it is a mistake to seek to locate the ethical aspect of the work solely or even primarily in these remarks; Wittgenstein, after all, implies that this aspect is something that is supposed to be made manifest by the text *as a whole.*[39]

It seems, then, that rather than viewing ethics as an additional subject matter treated by the *Tractatus,* for Wittgenstein we must come to understand in a new light what we've *already* been doing in reading this text. We must come to see the dialectical grappling with the limits of sense *as* a fundamentally ethical struggle. The attempt to make apparent this dimension of Wittgenstein's thought will occupy us in the last chapter of this book. Our aim here will not be to sum up and explain the "real meaning" of the text (although the temptation to do so will be especially strong at this point), but only to bring out explicitly what, for Wittgenstein, is properly an internal feature of philosophical inquiry.

V

One further set of questions needs to be addressed before we turn to the details of the text. These concern the inevitable demand for a more complete justification of our approach to the *Tractatus.* Why *must* we take the difficulties in rendering the text coherent (discussed in Section II) to indicate the need for reading it in the dialectical manner that is here being urged? Is it not just this kind of incoherence that motivates the fundamental shift in Wittgenstein's thought? Indeed, doesn't our approach have the consequence of collapsing the distinction between the early and later thinker – the distinction that Wittgenstein himself time and again remarks on?

To the first question, the honest answer is a perhaps disappointing one: *nothing* ultimately compels one to read the *Tractatus* in the way that I maintain. This, however, I do not take to be a shortcoming of my particular approach, but a feature of any interpretation of a philosophical work (a point, I believe, that Wittgenstein himself would insist on). For at issue are fundamental intuitions about what *kind* of thinker Wittgenstein at bottom really is – not straightforward "mistakes" settled through the production of "proof text." The legitimacy of our own particular approach can then only be established – or fail to be established – in a wholesale manner, through its ability to deal with the details of the text in a compelling manner, to render the whole coherent. That, of course, is not to claim that such an ability functions as a *criterion* of our interpretation's adequacy. (The assertion that a reading is acceptable *because* it renders the text more coherent is really no more than a grammatical remark in the sense of the later Wittgenstein.) Rather, I am simply saying that, in the end, our interpretation, like any textual interpretation, must wear its persuasiveness on its face.

The other objections must be met more forcefully. For it is quite reasonable to demand that a comprehensive interpretation be able to accommodate Wittgenstein's many post-Tractarian references to shifts in his thinking; if our reading has the consequence that such remarks must simply be dismissed, it cannot be entirely convincing. Let me be clear, then, that I by no means wish to downplay the significance of Wittgenstein's claims to have changed his mind on various matters. On the contrary, one of the subaims of this study is just to shed some light on this whole issue. What I shall seek to show, in general, is that Wittgenstein's later self-criticisms are to be understood as the recognition in his own thinking of the very philosophical demons the *Tractatus* had sought to completely exorcise. These criticisms do not take the form of a global reassessment of his overall philosophical aims but, rather, shifts in his understanding of rather specific points – the analogy between a proposition and a picture, the role of the quantifier, the nature of analysis, and so forth.

Of course, the very specificity of these criticisms has led many commentators to understand them as revisions to a general philosophical *theory*. Why would Wittgenstein be concerned with such details if he were truly committed to the ultimate nonsensicality of the questions at issue?[40] But I believe that we are here presented with a false dichotomy. And, indeed, from what we have said above it might already be apparent just why this is the case – that is, why matters of detail will loom large for Wittgenstein, even while his fundamental philosophical orientation remains the same. For if, as I maintain, "nonsense" is not a general or self-standing predicate for the *Tractatus*, if, that is, the assertion that such and such a claim does not make sense is related internally to the particular *way* its incoherence is made manifest, then a precise characterization of the nature of that incoherence is all-important. To misdescribe the philosophical problem is in a sense to miss the point – Wittgenstein's own (real) point – entirely; it is to propagate the very confusions from which Wittgenstein aims to liberate us.[41]

For Wittgenstein, much will therefore be at stake in eliminating what he comes to regard as the distortions in the *Tractatus'* presentation of the appropriate perspective – hence the dire character that he often attributes to the "errors" in his early thought. In the course of this study, we shall then address some of these later corrections, and seek to understand them in light of our reading of the *Tractatus*. And while these points about Wittgenstein's development will in general be made in the footnotes, this should by no means be taken as indicating their lesser importance; the issue of the interplay between the early and late philosopher instead informs our reading throughout.

In what follows, we shall be immersed in very close textual analysis of the *Tractatus*. The focus required to work through the internal intricacies of this difficult text will preclude our offering a great many remarks as we go along about the broader project in which Wittgenstein is engaged; that broader project, one hopes, will emerge through the details. And while I recognize that this sort of approach places a high demand on the reader, I believe it to be very much in the spirit of the philosopher at the center of our study.

CHAPTER I

PICTURES AND LOGICAL ATOMISM

I

The *Tractatus* opens with the famous declaration: "The world is everything that is the case" (TLP 1), followed by the qualification: "The world is the totality of facts (*Tatsachen*), not of things" (TLP 1.1). One is immediately struck by the dogmatic, absolutely authoritative tone of these claims. We do not at once know why they have been offered up, or what the basis for asserting them might be, nor will any later justifications be provided. They present themselves, in the words of the Preface, as "unassailable and definitive" (TLP p. 28) – beyond reproach it seems, but also, perhaps, beyond proof. What is the stance of the *Tractatus?* From what position are its absolute pronouncements made?

One might suppose that such self-reflective questions would have little relevance to the opening of the *Tractatus.* The text at this point looks entirely outward, on to the world; any concern with the conditions of its own utterance apparently falls outside of its purview. It is as if the author of the *Tractatus* were completely absorbed into the external reality that is here described – as if Wittgenstein were, so to speak, presenting a realist's perspective purely realistically. If that is the case, however, we must recognize that this cannot *itself* be an unself-conscious move on his part. For at 5.634, after denying that there is an "*a priori* order of things," he remarks: "Here it can be seen that solipsism, when its implications are followed out strictly, coincides with pure realism. The self of solipsism shrinks to a point without extension, and there remains the reality co-ordinated with it" (TLP 5.64). "Realism" and "solipsism" (a term that, for Wittgenstein, is often used synonymously with what we would ordinarily call "idealism") do not refer to competing philosophical positions but, rather, to equivalent ways of describing the world. Unless we are to imagine him to shift radically his thinking in the course of the book, Wittgenstein cannot then be understood as at the start straightforwardly *advocating* a realist stance in opposition to some other philosophical position.[1] Instead, it seems more accurate to see the opening as one means of characterizing or exemplifying a perspective: the *Tractatus* is attempting to adopt completely a certain way of looking at the world in order to make manifest what that outlook comes to. And that suggests that, far from dismissing all questions about the nature of its own stance, this text from the very beginning brings such questions to the fore.

The occurrence of the word "logic" at 2.012 and 2.0121 would then appear to be significant. "In logic nothing is accidental: if a thing can occur in an atomic fact the possibility of that atomic fact must already be prejudged in the thing" (TLP 2.012). "Nothing in the province of logic can be merely possible. Logic deals with every possibility, and all possibilities are its facts" (TLP 2.0121). Wittgenstein is not here describing a subject from afar but, rather, referring to the very activity in which he is engaged: the *Tractatus* is itself a logical inquiry, the perspective it adopts is the perspective of logic. This already begins to throw light on the reasons for the text's peculiar, seemingly dogmatic style. For a logical inquiry, as Wittgenstein conceives of it, would appear to be essentially different from a scientific investigation. While a scientific investigation seeks to determine what is the case, logic deals only with the possibility of what is the case. The limits of logic are the limits of the possible. This suggests not only that it can make no sense to speak of anything beyond logic but also that it makes no sense to speak of new domains *within* logic, of logical *discoveries*. The full expanse of logic must, in some sense, already be present to us. A book on logic should not then contain arguments, as if it described novel facts about whose existence we had to be convinced. Rather, one's only concern can be to lay matters out perspicuously, to present things in such a way as to allow us to, as it were, recall what we already know. The apparent dogmatism of the *Tractatus* reflects just the utterly uncontroversial nature of the subject with which it deals.

The aim of the present chapter is then to bring out how the *Tractatus'* "ontological remarks" (TLP 1–2.063), as well as the first part of the picture theory, serve to clarify this "uncontroversial subject," to begin to make fully evident the real character of a logical inquiry. Now such an interpretation might seem difficult to sustain, given that, a few scattered comments notwithstanding, "logic" as we ordinarily conceive of it – that is, as it is systematically presented in, say, Frege's *Begriffsschrift* or Russell's *Principia Mathematica* – is not treated by Wittgenstein until the 3s or even the 4s. Should we not then say that the early discussion is merely preparatory, or that it serves, as Mounce suggests, only to delineate how the world must be if there are propositions and hence the possibility of logic?[2] While these suggestions may sound tempting, I claim that they rest on too narrow a conception of what, for Wittgenstein (or, indeed, for Frege and Russell), logic consists in. To be sure, the *Tractatus* does in one sense distinguish mathematical logic from the attempt to give a broader account *of* that endeavor: this distinction is reflected in the text's application of the term "senseless" (*sinnlos*) to expressions of the form "p v ~p," but "nonsensical" (*unsinnig*) to expressions like "p is a proposition."[3] Nonetheless, as we shall see, mathematical logic is critiqued only insofar as it answers to the interests of logic in the broader sense – that is, insofar as it is put forward in the service of something like a Fregean project of spelling out the "laws of thought." It is always this inquiry into the fundamental possibilities of sense and nonsense that is of concern to Wittgenstein in the *Tractatus,* and it is this that will represent our concern as well.

II

We can now begin to reflect in more detail on the fact/thing distinction with which the text begins. Wittgenstein, in a later conversation with Desmond Lee, offers this interpretation of the *Tractatus'* opening remarks: "The world does not consist of a catalogue of things and facts about them (like a catalogue of a show). . . . What the world is is given by description and not by a list of objects" (CL 119). We might imagine a world consisting of objects a and b and a relation R. If our aim is to describe accurately this world, it is not enough simply to offer a list of these constituents – this list would not distinguish a universe in which aRb is the case from one in which bRa is the case. Instead, our description must incorporate within it some acknowledgment of structure; it must see the world as composed of facts, not things. Given the above discussion, however, it would appear that the focus of *logic* cannot be on this structure, the obtaining of *Tatsachen* as such. For as 1.21 states (and 2.061 reiterates), facts are logically independent of one another: "Any [Tatsache] can either be the case or not be the case, and everything else remain the same" (TLP 1.21). Whether fact A obtains or does not obtain is then a contingent matter that is irrelevant to the perspective of the *Tractatus*. Logic's concern, it would seem, must only be with the *possibility* of the *Tatsachen*, with what conditions their obtaining or not obtaining.

It is in connection with this idea that the notion of the object (*Gegenstand*) must initially be understood. For, given what is held at 2 and 2.01, one might otherwise wonder how the original primacy of fact over thing is to be maintained. "What is the case, the fact (*Tatsache*) is the existence of atomic facts (*Sachverhalten*) (TLP 2). An atomic fact is a combination of objects (entities [*Sachen*], things [*Dingen*])" (TLP 2.01). The difficulty is that if these remarks are taken to mean that a fact is made up of atomic facts and an atomic fact is made up of objects or things or entities (Wittgenstein makes it clear here that these terms are interchangeable), then it appears that the world is, at bottom, composed of things not facts after all; we are back to conceiving of reality as describable by a list. It would seem, then, that while the primacy of facts may not preclude all talk of objects, neither can the latter be understood as a more basic constituent of the world. Instead, as becomes apparent when we reflect on the above conception of logic, "fact" and "object" must be seen as standing at different levels: one's hold on the notion of an object comes through a *way of approaching* what is the case, through looking at a series of facts with an eye to what is common to them. To identify the objects is then not literally to further decompose the world but, rather, to seek to grasp its logical basis, the condition of its possibility.[4]

Indeed, the notion of possibility is bound up with the *Tractatus'* initial account of the object:

> Just as we cannot think of spatial objects at all apart from space, or temporal objects apart from time, so we cannot think of *any* object apart from the possibility of its connexion with other things.
> If I can think of an object in the context of an atomic fact, I cannot think of it apart from the *possibility* of this context. (TLP 2.0121)
> If I know an object, then I also know all the possibilities of its occurrence in atomic facts.

(Every such possibility must lie in the nature of the object.)
A new possibility cannot subsequently be found. (TLP 2.0123)

The point might be put as follows. It is constitutive of the object to occur in an atomic fact, but not only in *this* fact; the object is understood just through its appearance in a whole series of facts and in this sense can be said to represent the "possibility" of any one of them. This is not, however, to suggest that the Tractarian object must therefore be understood as dissolving simply into a possibility – as if we could understand the condition of the world apart from any consideration of how things actually stand. Instead, the object is this thing taken against the background of all the rest of its possibilities of combination with other things. If "form" is understood, as 2.033 suggests, as the "possibility of structure," then the object is not form alone, but, just as is stated of substance at 2.025, both form *and* content.[5]

It is useful to compare this conception of the object with Frege's. Frege famously draws a distinction between the object and the function – roughly, between that which corresponds to a proper name and the "unsaturated," predicative entity that combines with it. He emphasizes the way in which the function does not stand on its own but is instead given by looking to what is common to a series of propositions. Thus, he suggests that the real nature of the function could be made apparent through the use of blank spaces for the argument place of a functional expression, as when the expression "$2x^3 + x$" is written as "$2(\ )^3 + (\ )$." But while Frege goes on to contrast this idea of a "dependent" function with that of an object as a self-standing entity, one that is a "whole complete in itself,"[6] the *Tractatus'* aim would seem to be to bring out how no genuine logical distinction could be drawn between these notions; both function and (Fregean) object must be equally understood in terms of their capacity to occur in a space of facts. In this vein Wittgenstein remarks: "The thing is independent, insofar as it can occur in all *possible* states of affairs, but this form of independence is a form of connexion with the atomic fact, a form of dependence" (TLP 2.0122). Thus, too, he asserts in the *Notebooks:* "Relations and properties, etc. are objects too" (NB 61).

It seems that we should then say that Wittgensteinian objects comprise Frege's objects, as well as his first-order functions, second-order functions, and so forth. Of course, since these Fregean categories are set up in such a way as to be applicable to anything whatsoever that can be said about the world, this cannot be altogether incorrect. But insofar as putting matters this way makes it appear that Wittgenstein is riding roughshod over Frege's more fine-grained distinctions, this formulation is misleading. For it is essential to recognize that the *Tractatus* is not at the start attempting to tell us what sorts of things there are; to introduce the notion of an object is not yet to have identified a logical *kind*. On the contrary, Wittgenstein's emphasis on combinatorial possibilities is meant to question the coherence of such *a priori* categorization: *what* a given object is is only determined by the specific range of its occurrences in atomic facts, that which 2.0141 calls the "form of the object." Thus he remarks:

> Two objects of the same logical form are – apart from their external properties – only differentiated from one another in that they are different. (TLP 2.0233) Either a thing has properties which no other has, and then one can distinguish it straight away from the others by a description and refer to it; or, on the other hand, there are several things which have the totality of their properties in common, and then it is quite impossible to point to any one of them.
>
> For if a thing is not distinguished by anything, I cannot distinguish it – for otherwise it would be distinguished. (TLP 2.02331)

We have no way of establishing the identity of an object except through its particular capacities to combine with other objects. To attempt to differentiate two objects with the same logical form is to do no more than to make a bare assertion of difference, a claim with no content.

Still, one might wonder how the question of separating two objects of the same logical form could initially arise, even in principle. Would this not be like trying to ask whether this desk might be distinguished from itself? We again recall, though, that objects are not merely form, but both form and content. It now begins to become apparent that Tractarian objects defy easy integration not only into a Fregean framework, but also into any sort of traditional philosophical framework. While we will no doubt be tempted to bring to bear notions like "particular," "universal," or "sense datum" to try to make sense of what he has in mind,[7] Wittgenstein will not allow us to rely on any such categories as basic, as clarificatory. Indeed, it would appear to be the reverse: rather than seeking to understand objects in terms of some prior philosophical category, the *Tractatus* is suggesting that it is only through their possibilities of occurrence that those fundamental categories emerge. The object is, we might say, a primitive notion.[8]

With this point in mind, we can then begin to understand the so-called argument for simples (2.02–2.0212), a series of remarks that has received a good deal of treatment in the literature.[9] It is useful to quote this difficult passage in its entirety:

> The object is simple. (TLP 2.02)
> Every statement about complexes can be analyzed (*zerlegen*) into a statement about their constituent parts, and into those propositions which completely describe the complexes. (TLP 2.0201)
> Objects form (*bilden*) the substance of the world. Therefore they cannot be compound. (TLP 2.021)
> If the world had no substance, then whether a proposition had sense would depend on whether another proposition was true. (TLP 2.0211)
> It would then be impossible to form a picture of the world (true or false). (TLP 2.0212)

If we take these remarks on their face, Wittgenstein could well seem to be adopting some variety of Russellian "logical atomism." Like Russell in *The Philosophy of Logical Atomism,* he assumes the possibility of engaging in a process of logical analysis, a process that is imagined eventually to terminate in entities entirely lacking in complexity. Such simple objects constitute the substance of the world, its necessarily existent logical core. But whereas Russell is then naturally led to specify the nature of these endpoints of analysis – for him, logical atoms comprise particulars, relations, and qualities – Wittgenstein, we have just suggested, is essentially concerned to call into question the legitimacy of this kind of *a priori* logical categorization. A very different conception of simplicity would thus appear to be operating in the *Tractatus.*

If we are to bring out the real force of the Tractarian "argument for simples," we must then approach this passage with some care. Let us first focus on the idea of the "complex," which appears in 2.0201. It is important to compare what that remark says about the notion with 3.24, a claim that closely parallels 2.0201:

> A proposition about a complex stands in internal relation to the proposition about its constituent part.
> A complex can only be given by its description, and this will either be

> right or wrong. The proposition in which there is mention of a complex, if this does not exist, becomes not nonsense but simply false. (TLP 3.24)

In holding that a statement about a nonexistent complex is false rather than nonsensical, Wittgenstein is saying that the existence of that complex is irrelevant to the statement's sense. And while we are by no means yet in a position where we can discuss in detail the *Tractatus'* conception of analysis,[10] this claim, when taken together with 2.0211, implies at the very least that analysis must involve something other than a process of decomposing complex *objects* into their basic constituents. After all, if some complex C were imagined to be an entity literally made up of simple objects a and b, then C's nonexistence would entail the nonexistence of a and b. But since 2.0211 holds that the existence of objects is a condition of the possibility of sense, then the proposition that makes mention of (nonexisting) C becomes nonsensical. Again, though, that runs counter to 3.24.

By beginning to reflect on what it would mean to give an analysis, then, we are led to draw a fundamental distinction between the complex and the object. To make that distinction evident can now be seen to be the central purpose of 2.0201. Wittgenstein maintains there that a proposition about a complex can be analyzed into a statement about that complex's constituents, and this statement into a number of propositions that then completely describe that complex. Now a more complete account of exactly what procedure he has in mind at this point must await our discussion in the next chapter. Already, though, this remark can be seen to bring out how the complexity of the complex, so to speak, is ultimately (i.e., on completion of an analysis) absorbed into a series of propositions. The complex, in other words, is not to be treated, from a logical perspective, as one kind of entity among others in the world, one whose composition is essential to its nature. Instead, the very possibility of *describing* such an entity shows that it is really not an entity at all, but a structure – the obtaining or holding of entities.[11] For Wittgenstein, the apparent "reference" to a complex in the unanalyzed proposition marks a disguised allusion to a fact or set of facts.[12]

But if complexity is in this way always associated with the holding of facts, it then would appear that the object cannot *but* be simple – that there are no logical objects or entities other than simple ones.[13]

And, indeed, on reflection, we see that this point follows from the conception of the Tractarian object as constituted by its possibilities of combining with other things. For this is just to maintain that an object shorn of some of its combinatorial possibilities – that is, an object that is further decomposed – will no longer be the same entity. Wittgenstein, in holding at 2.021 that objects as the substance of the world "cannot be compound," must ultimately be understood as suggesting that predicating complexity of a logical entity can make no sense.

The contrast of the *Tractatus'* logical atomism with the Russellian version thus becomes striking. For Russell, the goal of logical analysis is to specify the sorts of objects that satisfy certain conditions: we identify the genuine simples when we distinguish from complex entities those objects that are incapable of definition and are instead known only by direct "acquaintance." In the *Tractatus,* though, our proper aim is not to seek the right *kinds* of *entities,* but rather to reveal clearly the logical role or function of that which is before us; logic, we might say, views the world always through the lens of simplicity. Wittgensteinian analysis must then be seen purely as an attempt to describe the world in such a way as to render perspicuous its simple, logical core. Thus, Wittgenstein remarks in the *Notebooks:*

> If, e.g., I call some rod "A" and a ball "B," I can say that A is leaning against the wall, but not B. Here the internal nature of A and B comes into view.
> A name designating an object thereby stands in a relation to it which is wholly determined by the logical kind of the object and which characterizes that logical kind.

Again, it is assumed that the identity of the object, as far as logic is concerned, is determined by the possibilities of its occurrence in a series of atomic facts. If we are to adopt the point of view of logic, it must then be evident from the role of the name in any given context alone just *what* the object it designates is – no additional contexts of its occurrence need be considered. So, for example, if "A" in the passage above were a genuine name, then A would appear in the atomic fact as *leaning* or even, perhaps, as leaning against a wall. It could not also occur as, say, a colored object, or something with a weight; that is, it could not have any such form and remain A. Solely from the functioning of the name "A" in the elementary proposition representing that atomic fact, the essential nature of this object becomes manifest.

We now can begin to see why Wittgenstein insists on the existence of that "substance" that the simple objects are said to form or constitute. For what would it mean to suppose that there might not be objects in this sense? It is useful to compare such a scenario with the possible nonexistence of a complex. As we saw above, 3.24 maintains that a proposition that makes mention of a nonexisting complex is false rather than nonsensical. If we understand talk of a "complex" as reflecting the confusion of a gesture toward a structure with a reference to a logically compound *entity,* the reason for this claim becomes apparent: the nonexistence of a complex is equivalent to the nonobtaining of a fact or series of facts. But the situation is otherwise with regard to an object. In denying that a genuine name has reference, we are not raising the possibility that one occurrence of an object does not exist – that is simply to imagine the nonobtaining of some atomic fact. Instead, given the *Tractatus'* conception of the object, what here would be suggested is that a whole *space* of possible occurrences might not be given. In Fregean terms, it would be as if one were to suppose not that a function did not hold for some argument, but that the argument place itself, the possibility of an argument, were not available. To deny the existence of substance is to call into question the very possibility of the representation of atomic facts.

Wittgenstein suggests that it is nonsensical to imagine such a possibility. The denial of substance, he claims, is tantamount to making the sense of a proposition dependent on the truth of another proposition. This is just to say that if the possibilities of representation were not already secured in advance, it would always be an open question as to whether a given fact *could* be represented. Without the givenness of objects, we would not be able to say that, for example, A is leaning against the wall until we first knew that A was the kind of thing that was capable of occurring in this context. But since the proposition expressing that knowledge would be subject to the same indefiniteness of sense, an infinite regress would then ensue. And in this case, as 2.0121 maintains, it would be impossible to form a picture of the world, true or false.

Notice, then, that the point here does not, as some commentators have suggested, turn on a worry over the holding of the connection between the name and the object – as if Wittgenstein were claiming that, without a guarantee of immediate contact between language and the world, it would never be certain as to whether our names really did refer.[14] No such problem of reference is at issue in the *Tractatus*. For Wittgenstein, instead, the real concern is with the fundamental ascriptions that can be made to the world, the *possibilities* that allow the facts to stand in the way they do. The requirement for substance is ultimately nothing but the insistence that nothing underlies or conditions logic, that logic is, as it were, self-subsistent.[15] It is just this idea that is expressed in the characterization of substance as "what exists independently of what is the case" (TLP 2.024).

Now, it is not yet clear how this claim about the need for the logical possibilities of the world to be given in advance coheres with what we have said to be Wittgenstein's questioning of any attempt at *a priori* logical categorization; this tension only begins to resolve itself in the account of the picture. But the above discussion does allow us to gain a better grasp on the notion of the atomic fact:

> The object is the fixed, the existent; the configuration is the changing, the variable. (TLP 2.0271)
> The configuration of the objects forms the atomic fact. (TLP 2.0272)
> In the atomic fact objects hang in another, like the links of a chain. (TLP 2.03)

The atomic fact is in its essence an arrangement of objects. To say that these objects hang in one another like the links of a chain is to emphasize that no further elements are involved in this configuration, no additional "relations" to bind together its components: the atomic fact is constituted solely by the objects being arranged in *this* way. That particular arrangement 2.032 terms the "structure" of the *Sachverhalt;* the structure thus consists in *how* the objects hang together. Of course, since the identity of the object is determined by all its possibilities of combining, any single occurrence of an object – any particular way of its hanging in an atomic fact – does not exhaust its nature. But from the above preliminary points about analysis, it would seem that this nature (the form of the object) should nonetheless at least be evident through any one of those occurrences. In other words, the particular way that the object *does* lie in the atomic fact must reveal clearly just how it *can* lie – which is to say, what, from a logical perspective, it essentially is. 2.033 describes "form" as "the possibility of structure." The atomic fact, one could say, presents its structure precisely in such a way as to make the forms of its constituents manifest.

It thus becomes apparent that the requirement for objects and the postulation of atomic facts are closely linked; both, it would seem, are demands of the logical inquiry itself. To postulate the possibility of describing what is the case (the totality of *Tatsachen*) in terms of the existence of atomic facts is simply to suppose the possibility of a perspicuous presentation of the logical dimension of the world, its necessarily existent core. At the same time, however, reflection on this idea begins to reveal the peculiar nature of the inquiry into that "existent core." For it would appear that, even in the atomic fact, substance is presented only indirectly, emerging *through* the structure, through the way in which things stand. Rather than constituting an ordinary subject with its own special area of concern, then, the inquiry into substance seems ultimately to represent no more than a perspective on the world, a *way* of viewing what is the case. And that would suggest that, already, the *Tractatus* is leading us to call into question the fundamental supposition of the thought of Frege and Russell – the supposition that logic constitutes a genuine science.

Still, it must be acknowledged that the real nature of the question that the *Tractatus* is pursuing remains at this point abstract, indistinct. It is, I claim, the central aim of the subsequent discussion of the picture to bring that question – the fundamental question of logic – into sharper focus.[16] Of course, such an interpretation runs counter to the standard way of approaching the "picture theory" (so-called). On the standard view, the introduction of the picture represents the *Tractatus'* shift from ontology to the concern with language, the concern that occupies the text from that point on.[17] But while it is undeniable that the notion of the picture is meant to shed light on the proposition – propositions are explicitly described as pictures at 4.01 – it is not so clear that such a focus represents a genuine departure from the focus at the opening of the text. Certainly the *Notebooks* does not recognize a sharp distinction between an investigation into the proposition and an investigation into the world: "My *whole* task consists in explaining the nature of the proposition. That is to say, in giving the nature of all facts, whose picture the proposition *is*. In giving the nature of all being" (NB 39). Similarly, several remarks in the *Tractatus* appear to emphasize how the text's early claims about the world can be interchanged with points about language:

> The thing is independent, in so far as it can occur in all *possible* circumstances, but this form of independence is a form of connexion with the atomic fact, a form of dependence. (It is impossible for words to occur in two different ways, alone and in the proposition.) (TLP 2.0122)
> A spatial object must lie in infinite space. (A point in space is an argument place.) (TLP 2.0131)

Indeed, when we reflect on our own interpretation of the opening passages, we note how it also has been bound up with linguistic notions – how the notions of fact, object, and atomic fact have been explicated only through talk of propositions and names. This intertwining of the putatively independent notions of language and world would thus seem to be intrinsic to the *Tractatus'* understanding of the logical perspective. And this suggests that rather than marking a sudden shift in the direction of the text, the account of the picture is really only a deepening, a clarification of the same inquiry that is initiated at the start.

III

In keeping with this overall approach, we can then understand the introduction of the notion of the picture as immediately motivated by certain tensions in the remarks that close the 2.0s. First, we note the seemingly shifting sense of the term "world." In 2.04, "the world" is identified with the totality of *existent* atomic facts (*die Gesamtheit der bestehen den Sachverhalte*). Given the text's initial association of the world with all that is the case (TLP 1), all that is the case with the totality of facts (TLP 1.1), and this totality with the existence of atomic facts (TLP 2), we might have assumed that the totality of existent atomic facts constitutes the limit of the world. The subsequent introduction of the term "reality," a notion with an apparent wider extension than "the world," then comes as a surprise: "The existence *and nonexistence* of atomic facts is the reality" (TLP 2.06; italics mine). Is Wittgenstein imagining atomic facts that lie outside of the world? The idea is in itself strange enough. But it would also seem to blur the *Tractatus'* fundamental distinction between the fact as what happens to obtain and the object as its logical condition. For it is very tempting to view the nonexistent atomic fact – the fact that is not but could be – as in some sense *another* condition of the possibility of the (existent) atomic fact. Or, equally complicating matters, we may maintain the distinction between a fact and its condition, but then feel driven to posit possible *objects* (possible possibilities as it were) as the logical bases of these nonexistent, merely possible facts.

Wittgenstein's position becomes still more puzzling when we look at the supposed further clarification of 2.06 provided by 2.063: "The total reality is the world" (TLP 2.063). The just introduced distinction between "reality" and "the world" is now apparently denied or in some sense overcome; the *Tractatus* would seem both to propose the existence of facts outside of the world and to imply that such an idea doesn't make any sense. Why this equivocation? What is the status of the "negative fact," as Wittgenstein refers to the nonexistent atomic fact at 2.06? It is, it would seem, some version of the ancient problem of the nature of "what is not" that confronts us at the close of the 2.06s.

A second tension in the remarks ending the 2.0s centers around the question of the relation between atomic facts. At 2.062, in keeping with the 1.21s claim of the logical independence of facts, Wittgenstein claims: "From the existence or nonexistence of an atomic fact we cannot infer the existence or nonexistence of another" (TLP 2.062). This assertion, however, would seem to run counter what is maintained just three remarks previously: "The totality of existent atomic facts also determines which atomic facts do not exist" (TLP 2.05). One wonders how one set of facts can "determine" a second set if these facts are entirely independent of each other. It might be tempting to suppose that Wittgenstein is introducing the possibility of a relation of determination distinct from one of logical *inference.* But that would fly in the face of 6.37: "A necessity for one thing to happen because another has happened does not exist. There is only *logical* necessity" (TLP 6.37). The solution, it then seems, is that we cannot view positive and negative atomic facts as separate or independent notions: we can infer the nonexistence of A from the existence of A (A "determines" ~A) just because, from the perspective of A, ~A does not count as *another* fact.

Once more, then, we run up against the intrinsically ambiguous status of what is not. It now appears that this difficulty is connected with the notion of logical inference: the possibility of logical relations between facts, of a "reality" that extends beyond the limits of the world, and of nonexistent *Sachverhalten* are all closely linked. It is through the picture theory that we begin to see how this cluster of notions relates to the attempt to understand the unchanging substance at the heart of the world.

The move to a discussion of pictures is initiated abruptly, without any explanation: "We make to ourselves pictures of facts" (TLP 2.1). It is important to note at once the emphasis here on picturing as an activity: we *make* pictures of facts and to *ourselves*, for our own purposes. From the beginning, it would seem, Wittgenstein is viewing the picture not as an autonomous, self-interpreting entity, but rather as something to be viewed within the context of its use.[18] This emphasis is made even more explicit by Wittgenstein in a later conversation about the *Tractatus* with Waismann. After suggesting that the *Tractatus'* notion of a picture was used to highlight certain important features of a proposition, Wittgenstein goes on: "I could also use a measuring-rod as a symbol, that is, insert a measuring-rod into a description and use it in the same way as a proposition. You may even say, In many respects a proposition behaves just like a measuring-rod, and therefore I might just as well have called propositions measuring-rods" (VC 185). To speak of a measuring-rod is of course to speak of something that cannot be understood apart from its connection with human purposefulness – presumably no one will suppose that a ruler might apply itself to the object to be measured. We note, then, that the *Tractatus* does in fact at 2.1512 draw the analogy between a *picture* and a measuring rod (*Masstab*). The above passage would appear to suggest – and our later discussion will make clear – that the comparison is to be taken quite seriously, that it gives us the aspect of the picture that is crucial for Wittgenstein's whole account.

The significance of this emphasis on the picture as it is used is not yet apparent. But we shall see how some such idea will be essential in making sense of the next several remarks. First, then, 2.11: "The picture presents (*vorstellt*)[19] the states of affairs (*Sachlage*) in logical space, the existence and nonexistence of atomic facts (*Sachverhalten*)" (TLP 2.11). The reference here to "logical space" recalls 1.13: "The facts (*Tatsachen*) in logical space are the world." From the start, it would seem, the world is understood always against a larger – logical – backdrop of what is not the case.[20] Still, taken as it stands, 2.11 makes the problem of nonexistent facts seem yet more mysterious. How could the picture considered in itself *present* a negative fact? Is what is not present in the picture imagined also to be part of what it presents? The elements of the picture stand for (*vertreten;* "go proxy for") things (TLP 2.131), but this seems to say nothing about the possibility of representing facts that do not exist, or at least that do not exist in the configuration presented by the picture.

It is 2.15 that allows us to begin to understand the fundamental direction of Wittgenstein's account: "That the elements of the picture are combined (*verhalten*) with one another in a definite way presents (*vorstellt*) that the things are so combined with one another." The picture, as 2.141 states, is a fact and it would seem to be just this "facticity" that allows it to portray. Now clearly Wittgenstein is here implicitly challenging Frege's assimilation of a proposition to a name, as is often noted:[21] propositions as pictorial *facts* must be sharply distinguished from names, which, as analogues to the pictorial elements, serve only as proxies for objects. But it is essential to understand the real purpose of Wittgenstein's attack on the Fregean conception. For the temptation amongst commentators is to suggest, even while pointing out Wittgenstein's difference with Frege, that the *Tractatus* is here ultimately concerned with the problem of how some particular picture fact can be connected with the appropriate world fact. Thus, Black, for example, sees the picture theory as an attempt to give an account of how the relational proposition "aRb" could mean that some *specific* state of affairs cSd obtains.[22] To state the problem in this way, however, is just to reiterate the Fregean construal of the proposition (picture) as a kind of name (i.e., pictorial element). It is to view the sense of the picture as something to which the picture *corresponds,* a kind of entity to which that picture must somehow be securely fastened. And, indeed, we can now see how such a Fregean view is connected with the perplexity over the issue of negative facts. For on this conception we are naturally led to wonder what it is that can constitute the reference of pictures that depict facts that do not obtain. It is then a short step – a step not actually taken by Frege himself, but one toyed with by Russell[23] – to begin postulating a special domain of nonexistent facts, a shadowy realm of all that *is* not but *could* be.

Wittgenstein's emphasis on the facticity of the picture is in part meant to get at the confusion that would bring us to make such a move. Rather than leading us to imagine picturing as a relation between a new kind of entity – facts – we are urged to see that no real relation is at issue in the first place. Wittgenstein states that it is just *that* these proxies for objects stand to each other in the way they do that says things in the world so stand. This is meant to bring out that what is doing the expressing cannot be the set of pictorial proxies as such, but rather our having *taken* these proxies as a certain kind of fact about the world. To speak meaningfully of the picture as a "model of reality" (TLP 2.12) thus presupposes understanding the picture within the context of its application; *the* picture, we might say, is in a certain sense an abstraction from the process of pictur*ing*. But then if our concern is to explain how the picture is, as it were, articulate, how it can express something about the world, it becomes apparent that talk of reference is completely beside the point. For what we seek is not dependent on the existence or nonexistence of some entity, but is instead part of what it means to have a picture in the first place.

With this emphasis on the activity of picturing in place we can now better understand remark 2.11: "The picture presents (*vorstellt*) the states of affairs (*Sachlage*) in logical space, the existence and nonexistence of atomic facts (*Sachverhalten*)." In speaking there of what the picture "presents," Wittgenstein is conceiving of the picture in relation to all those atomic facts it can be *used* to represent. The picture presents the existence *and* nonexistence of atomic facts precisely because it is the same picture that allows us to say that some fact either is or is not the case. This idea Wittgenstein indeed comes back to over and over again in the *Notebooks*. Compare, for example, these remarks from November 1914:

> That two people are not fighting can be represented by representing them as not fighting and also by representing them as fighting and saying that the picture shows how things are *not*. We could represent by means of negative facts just as much as by means of positive ones. (NB 23)
>
> In order for it to be possible for a negative atomic fact (*Sachverhalt*) to be given, the picture of the positive atomic fact must be given. (NB 24)
>
> Negation refers to the *finished* sense of the negated proposition and not to its way of representing. If a picture represents what-is-not-the-case in the aforementioned way, this only happens through its representing *that* which *is* not the case. For the picture says, as it were: '*This* is how it

> is *not*', and to the question "How is it not?" just the positive proposition is the answer. (NB 25)

The point would seem to be to emphasize the way in which the negative fact is dependent on, or given entirely by means of, its positive counterpart. In conceiving of matters in this manner we will be far less tempted to reify the negative fact, to attribute to it some special ontological status. (And here we should recall Wittgenstein's initially suggesting that the negative fact lies in some sense outside the world.) At the same time, we see that from the point of view of logic there is nothing sacrosanct about the existent fact either; positive and negative fact stand on the same level, a contrast between two uses of a picture. (This was the point of Wittgenstein's identifying the total reality and the world at 2.063.) Positive and negative fact are coequal inhabitants of logical space, introduced together at 2.11.

The effect of this whole discussion is then to bring into sharper focus the question which Wittgenstein believes is really at stake in this context. In recognizing the interdependence of positive and negative fact, we see that our concern here must be to go, as it were, behind these facts, to account for the possibility of both together. That is, rather than attempting to explain how a particular picture can correctly designate some fact in the world, the *Tractatus* suggests that logic must properly inquire into the possibility of representation, true *or* false. The question that the picture theory begins to bring into relief is then the question Wittgenstein poses early on in the *Notebooks:* "What is the ground of our – certainly well founded – confidence that we shall be able to express any sense we like in our two-dimensional script?" (NB 6). What we want to explain ultimately, in other words, is how our propositions are capable of representing *all* and *only* states of affairs in the world, how it is that our propositions are guaranteed to make sense in the first place. But that is to say that what is really at issue here is just the question of the nature of the fundamental categories in terms of which the world is constituted – for the *Tractatus,* the question of the nature of substance itself. It is in the next several remarks that we see the core of Wittgenstein's response.

In the present context, then, the problem will have to do with giving some sort of specification of the possibility of the picture's "presenting" (in Wittgenstein's special sense of this term)[24] what it does. Now the possibility of the pictorial fact, of the particular determinate structure itself, the *Tractatus* calls the picture's "pictorial form" (*Form der Abbildung;* TLP 2.15). 2.151 states that this pictorial form is also the possibility of the things being related to each other in the same way. The pictorial fact and the world fact that it represents would thus seem to operate within the same space of possibility. And, indeed, just *that* this is the case is standardly taken to be the central contention of the picture theory.[25] Wittgenstein's answer to the question of how the picture – and hence language – can always be about the world is thus supposedly to be: they share a form.

Still, while I certainly do not deny that Wittgenstein speaks of something in common between the picture and what is pictured – this is explicitly asserted at 2.16 and 2.161 – the important question concerns his attitude toward this claim. In that regard, I insist that, as an *explanation* of how the picture is always capable of depicting the world, the strategy of taking recourse in talk of an isomorphism is empty; it amounts to no more than the claim that depicting the world is possible because the world has the possibility of being depicted. One might usefully compare Wittgenstein's approach here with the Russellian postulation of particulars, qualities, and relations as the ultimate "simples," or even with the Kantian attempt to specify the fundamental categories that constitute the phenomenal world. The *Tractatus'* assertion of the isomorphism between the picture and reality cannot be understood as an effort to offer the basis of an alternative answer to the ones provided by Russell and Kant but, rather, just as a way of expressing the *absence* of any such answer. This then implies that our proper aim here must be to understand how we are driven into making this empty assertion, why it is for Wittgenstein that we cannot at this level draw a meaningful distinction between the picture and what it depicts.[26]

Toward that end, let us first seek to become clearer on what it would mean to specify the picture's pictorial form. What is wanted, it would seem, is an account of the coordination of pictorial elements and objects referred to at 2.13 and 2.131, the coordination that 2.1514 terms the picture's "pictorial relationship" (*die abbildende Beziehung*). Now clearly one dimension of this correlation, the choice of particular pictorial representatives, is arbitrary: if my aim is to represent a book lying on a table, it is entirely up to me whether to use rectangles, squares, color patches or what have you to stand for the objects composing that fact. Wittgenstein, at 2.131, uses the term *vertreten* ("The elements of the picture stand [*vertreten*], in the picture, for the objects") to designate this connection between pictorial element (and, later, name) and thing; it is by means of the *vertreten* relation that what is earlier called the "content" of the object comes into view. But setting up this sort of arbitrary correlation would not by itself seem sufficient to ensure that any picture I construct will portray a possible state of affairs. What is to stop me from, for example, placing a pictorial representative of an event into a pictorial representative of a *hole*,[27] or picturing a situation in which red is *louder* than green? Evidently, the assuming of a particular outward appearance is not enough to guarantee that a set of correlated pictorial elements is a genuine picture in the *Tractatus'* sense of the term.[28] Only if the pictorial representatives have all the same possibilities of combination as their real world counterparts – only if they have the same form as those objects – will we say that they are *really* representatives of the latter. The legitimacy of the arbitrary correlations we set up would appear to depend in some sense on a deeper coordination of form.[29]

The *Form der Abbildung* has to do just with this idea of a non-arbitrary, inner connection of the picture and reality. As the possibilities of combination common to the pictorial elements and the objects they stand for, it constitutes the ultimate ground of our ability to picture the world. In laying bare the pictorial form, the forms of the objects, it then seems that we would come to see the *essence* of representation; that is, the *a priori* core both of our means of representing and of what is represented. And that is to say that the specification of the pictorial form would constitute a large step toward the fulfillment of one of the most fundamental tasks of philosophy, as traditionally conceived.

Wittgenstein's way of attempting to drain this whole inquiry of its philosophical allure – the basis of his "solution" to the problem of the nature of substance – begins to become apparent when we closely consider remarks 2.151 through 2.1512:

> The pictorial form is the possibility that the things are so combined with one another as are the elements of the picture. (TLP 2.151)
> *That* is how a picture is attached to reality; it reaches right out to it. (TLP 2.1511)
> It is laid against reality like a measure (*ein Masstab* – i.e., a ruler). (TLP 21512)

We must once more ask ourselves what it means to compare a picture with a ruler. A useful way of approaching this question is suggested by remarks 43 and 44 of the *Philosophical Remarks*. Here, after again stressing the importance of the picture-ruler comparison, Wittgenstein points out that the possibility of measuring in general does not presuppose a particular length for the object to be measured. All that is necessary is for me to have a way of using the ruler, of applying it to the world.[30] The *Tractatus* similarly suggests that the possibility of *depicting* in general does not assume the existence of some fact or other in the world, but only a way of picturing – a way of projecting our pictures. And since, as we have seen, our hold on the picture is parasitic on a notion of the picture in use, that method of projection can be said to be in a certain sense already given, once we are given the pictorial fact. It would then follow that a picture, simply in virtue of *being* a picture in the *Tractatus'* sense, *must* always present some possible state of affairs. This indeed is just what Wittgenstein suggests at 2.1513: "According to this view the pictorial relationship which makes it a picture also belongs to the picture." The point, in other words, is that what makes something into a picture of the *world* – the pictorial elements being correlated with the things they stand for – is also what makes it into a picture in the first place. Conceived in this way, a picture is seen to carry within it its inner coordinations with reality and thus cannot fail to depict.[31]

To say that the inner coordinations with reality are part of the picture, however, is at the same time to suggest the insubstantiality of the pictorial form. (As always in the *Tractatus,* the appearance of substantial necessity – in this case the necessity of the picture's attachment to the world – is a mark of one's failure to have made a genuine claim.) For what Wittgenstein's account is meant to bring out is that the essential possibilities of combination common to the pictorial elements and the objects are given, as it were, after the fact, precisely *through* the projection of the picture on to reality.[32] Rather than having an *a priori,* normative status, the pictorial form is parasitic on our way of picturing with a picture.

Wittgenstein's point can be brought into sharper focus if we reflect on the notion of space, one of the pictorial forms referred to at 2.171.[33] The above discussion is meant to get us to see the incoherence of supposing that in order to construct a spatial picture we must "have" beforehand a notion of space to function as a kind of constraint. It is not, in other words, as if in constructing a picture of, say, a book lying on a table, I must take care to have chosen proxies not only for these objects, but also for their capacity to assume spatial relations. Instead, that these objects are in space – their spatial form – is revealed through my being able to construct a picture in the first place: the fact that these two shapes can be correlated with that book and that table in such a way as to make a genuine picture *gives us* part of what we mean by "space." The limits of my ability to make a picture of this kind then constitute the limits of my notion of spatiality – which is to say that this pictorial form is not a constituent of a given picture, but part of its way of being related to the world, part of what this picture *is*. And that would seem to be just another way of stating the point of 2.172: "A picture, however, cannot depict its pictorial form: it shows it forth" (*weist sie auf*).

IV

The central Tractarian notion of showing is thus introduced at the crucial moment in the discussion of the picture. Viewed in isolation, this idea naturally leads us to imagine the existence of necessary, but ineffable features of reality. With the above considerations in mind, however, we see that the real aim of the *Tractatus* is to turn such an idea on its head; we see that the show/say distinction functions as part of the attempt to dissipate the urge to *look for* any such "necessary features." For it now becomes apparent that the assertion that the pictorial form can only be shown is equivalent to claiming that everything logic *would* want to say about the *a priori* nature of pictorial representation is a feature of how we operate with the picture. Rather than tantalizing us with the notion of an intrinsically inexpressible dimension to reality, the real point here is then to bring out the emptiness of the question motivating our whole inquiry. But notice that, without the demand put forward in that question, the idea that there is any contrast with "what can be said" has no role whatsoever. That is, to put it somewhat crudely, it is simply pointless to state as a general, self-standing claim either that something is or that something is not shown by this picture of a book lying on a table. Instead, the possibility of introducing this language is dependent on the logician's desire to get at the essence of representation, his sense that there is, in this respect, a gap in our understanding of the world; the show/say distinction, we might say, serves as a response to *him*.

We now begin to see more concretely what we described in the Introduction as the fundamentally "dialectical" nature of the *Tractatus'* argument – the way in which its central notions only have their life in relation to the philosophical temptations that the book aims to eradicate.[34] The point in the present context can be made still clearer if we consider for a moment a more standard interpretation of the role of the show/say distinction in the picture theory.[35] Such an approach tends to treat that which is shown by the picture as a kind of unstateable *presupposition* of what the picture represents. Pears provides a good illustration of this view:

> [Wittgenstein believed that] the possibility of saying some things in factual discourse depends on the actuality of other things which cannot be said. Then the analogy with pictures was used to illustrate the dependence of the sayable on the unsayable: a portrait relies on the projective geometry which links the canvas to the sitter, but it does not include a diagram of that linkage.[36]

One's immediate response here might be to wonder why a second picture could not be used to represent the linkage between the canvas and the sitter.[37] Pears's answer is that, while this is of course possible, any such picture would ultimately have to "pick out the same facts about the sitter and use the same method of projection in order to pick them out."[38] The link between the picture and the world thus must seemingly defy all attempts at being fully represented, at least in any sort of informative way. This implies, for Pears's Wittgenstein, a more general restriction on our language's capacity to represent: the picture theory is ultimately construed as suggesting the impossibility of giving "a complete account of the sense of any factual sentence."[39]

Now the question of just how the picture theory is to be extended to language in general we have yet to discuss. But already we can see the way in which Pears's reading assumes a quite substantial or robust conception of the "unsayable." The pictorial form, while somehow not capturable in any picture, nonetheless has "actuality" as a kind of deep fact on which the possibility of depicting more superficial facts ultimately "depends." To be sure, Pears will construe the necessary inexpressibility of the pictorial form as part of the *Tractatus'* attempt to place a limit on meaningful discourse. In this sense, he might well agree with my claim that the show/say distinction forms the heart of Wittgenstein's attack on the possibility of an inquiry into the essence of the world and its representation. But we must see that it would, in this case, constitute a very different sort of attack. After all, nothing about the Pears's construal of the picture theory suggests that there would be anything *nonsensical* about the attempt to give an articulation of pictorial form. At best, Wittgenstein could only show that we are incapable of adopting the sort of external vantage point from which a "complete" – and this presumably must mean nonredundant – depiction of the underlying, evidently quite real, ground of representation could be given. On the Pears reading, then, the picture theory would serve to present the logico-philosophical investigation into the ground of representation as fundamentally coherent, but as in the end unsatisfiable.

My claim, however, is that Wittgenstein's real focus is not on the satisfiability of logic's project, but on the possibility of coherently imagining such a project in the first place. The *Tractatus* holds that the picture "must have in common" with reality its pictorial form "in order to depict (*abbilden*) it – correctly or incorrectly – in the way that it does" (TLP 2.17). The temptation to which Pears succumbs is to suppose that the depicting relation – the relation between the picture and what it is in general directed toward[40] – is here being treated as somehow undergirded by the pictorial form: the pictorial form constitutes a mysterious third element, a kind of metaphysical glue linking the picture and reality. But we have seen that the actual purpose of the picture theory is just to lead us away from such a view. Far from being imagined as a third element, stateable or unstateable, the pictorial form is no element at all, but rather part of the picture's way of depicting. The picture "must" have in common with reality its particular pictorial form precisely because this form is *constituted* by this picture's application to the world – just as the possibilities of length are given through the ruler's use in measuring magnitudes. This, of course, is not to construe that form as a kind of full-bodied entity resting tantalizingly just beyond human reach, nor, indeed, to put forward any sort of "claim" that could coherently be challenged. Instead, the point only has force when we recognize in it the fundamental question of logic. Its purpose is served if we see that the inquiry in which we have thought ourselves to be engaged is predicated on imagining a kind of division between the essential possibilities of the world and the means by which these are represented. To acknowledge that the pictorial form can only be shown is to acknowledge the incoherence of the attempt to draw such a division.

Still, with the assertion of the inexpressibility of the pictorial form we have by no means exhausted the *Tractatus'* discussion of the picture. Wittgenstein goes on to introduce the notions of sense, truth and falsity, logical picture, and the "representing" – as opposed to the "presenting" – dimension of the picture; the significance of these notions must be explored. Moreover, we have yet to see exactly how the above account is meant to apply to the proposition, how the initial points about the picture, as well those about the world and the nature of objects, will appear within the context of a more explicitly "linguistic" discussion. It is to the latter issue that we shall turn in the next chapter.

CHAPTER II

WHAT IS ANALYSIS?

I

Wittgenstein's declaration of the inexpressibility of the pictorial form at 2.172 and 2.174 is followed by the introduction of a new notion – the logical form: "What every picture, of whatever form, must have in common with reality in order to be able to depict (*abbilden*) it at all – rightly or falsely – is the logical form (*die logische Form*), that is, the form of reality" (TLP 2.18). With this mention of "reality," we are of course called back to the discussion at the beginning of the picture theory. The notion of reality, we have seen, is connected with the existence and nonexistence of atomic facts, which is to say with everything that the picture can be used to depict. It is not at once clear, however, just how such an idea would differentiate the logical form from the pictorial, if Wittgenstein does in fact intend to distinguish the two. After all, the claim that the picture must share with the reality it depicts a *pictorial* form is central to the picture theory. What is the purpose of holding that there is also common to the picture and reality another kind of form?

The basis of Wittgenstein's answer is suggested by the next two remarks: "If the pictorial form is the logical form, then the picture is called a logical picture" (TLP 2.181). "Every picture is *also* a logical picture. (On the other hand, for example, not every picture is spatial.)" (TLP 2.182). On this account, the logical form appears in some sense to contain the pictorial form: every spatial picture is to be construed as a logical picture, but not every logical picture is spatial (or temporal or colored). "Logical form" is thus to be understood as a more general term for the representational possibilities of any picture. But if this is the case, the notion of pictorial form appears to become unnecessary; it seems we should call *all* pictures "logical" and speak only of logical form.[1] Or are we to assume, as Friedlander seems to, that "logical form" describes something not only more general, but also *additional* to the pictorial form – a feature of the picture on top of its *Form der Abbildung?*[2] The precise nature of the generalization that Wittgenstein here alludes to would appear to be somewhat of a mystery.

In fact, an adequate account of this generalization is in the end inseparable from an understanding of the *Tractatus'* view of the nature and purpose of logical analysis, of how fundamentally this view diverges from that of Frege and Russell. To gain such an understanding will constitute the chief purpose of the present chapter. We can, however, already begin to get a clearer idea of what is at stake in the introduction of the notion of logical form if we first recall the ultimate purpose of the picture theory – namely, to serve as a means of shedding light on the significant *proposition.* It then becomes apparent that Wittgenstein must somewhere address the obvious point that, as he puts it at 4.011, "at the first glance the proposition – say as it stands printed on paper – does not *seem* to be a picture of the reality of which it treats" (emphasis mine). The problem, in other words, is that, despite the detailed consideration of the nature of representation in the 2.1s, it is not immediately evident exactly how the *Tractatus'* remarks about the picture are to be extended to language in general. My suggestion, then, following Dreben, is that the notion of logical form is meant to ease this transition. That is, by generalizing the idea of form – by speaking not simply of what the picture must have in common with reality to depict it "in its particular way" (*seine Art und Weise;* TLP 2.17), but also of what it shares with reality in order to depict it *at all* – Wittgenstein can hope to get us to think of picturing in cases in which no literal structural resemblance is involved.[3] Thus, in reflecting on the thought or proposition as a "logical picture of the fact" (TLP 3), we will concern ourselves with the relation of picture and pictured only with regard to the bare possibility of their being logically linked, a possibility that is presumably contained in the more tangible connection between, say, a spatial representation and the corresponding fact.

Now just how we are to conceive of such a "bare possibility" is, of course, unclear. And indeed, although we might suppose the unclarity of this notion to be necessary, given the perspective the *Tractatus* ultimately aims to communicate, by the time of the *Philosophical Remarks* Wittgenstein seems to doubt whether the generalization of the picture can in any way be legitimately employed:[4]

> It's easy to understand that a ruler is and must be in the same space as the object measured by it. But in what sense are *words* in the same space as an object whose length is described in words, or in the same space as a color, etc.? It sounds absurd. (PR 45)

Here the very possibility of the analogy between pictorial and logical form is called into question. Nonetheless, even in this criticism we see what Wittgenstein implicitly regards as central in the *Tractatus'* extension of the notion of picturing. For in relying on the metaphor of the ruler, he is once more bringing to the fore the *application* of a particular method of representation. As in the account of the ordinary picture, then, logical picturing would seem to be approached with an eye to such application, with an eye to how "reality" in the Tractarian sense of the term, is structured through our specific way of describing it. The importance of this point will become apparent as we seek to elaborate the *Tractatus'* development of the idea of logical form.

II

Many of Wittgenstein's remarks about the proposition in the early 3s in fact closely parallel those about the picture. Thus, 3.14 – "What constitutes a propositional sign is that in it its elements (the words) stand in a determinate relation to one another" – mirrors 2.14 in phasizing the facticity of the propositional sign. 3.141, in referring to the propositional sign as "articulate" and as other than a mere "blend of words," brings to the fore the distinction between a fact and a name, just as was suggested in 2.15 with regard to the difference between picture and pictorial element. Indeed, the reliance on the earlier points about the picture is quite explicit at 3.1431: "The essential nature of the propositional sign becomes very clear when we imagine it made up of spatial objects (such as tables, chairs, books) instead of written signs. The mutual spatial position of these things then expresses the sense of the proposition." In reflecting on the way the elements of a spatial picture are related to each other, it would seem that we are meant to understand the *essence* of the proposition.

Now certain details of the *Tractatus'* view of the notion of sense will have to await treatment in the next chapter. But already we are in a position to approach the controversial and much discussed remark 3.1432: "We must not say, 'The complex sign *"aRb"* says *"a* stands in relation *R* to *b"*'; but we must say, '*That "a"* stands in a certain relation (*einer gewissen Beziehung*) to *"b"* says *that aRb*'." This remark is often held to suggest something about Wittgenstein's view of the unreality of properties and relations.[5] Thus, it is maintained, in a picture depicting a book lying on a table, the spatial relationship between the table and the book is not itself part of the picture, but, instead, is shown by the fact *that* these objects are related to each other in the way they are. In the same way, the argument goes, in the proposition expressing such a fact it is the relation of the *letter* "a" representing the book to the *letter* "b" representing the table that expresses the fact that aRb. "R" thus does not name anything; what it tries to represent is instead *shown* by "a" and "b" bearing to each other a certain relation. The thrust of 3.1432 is then to claim that relations (and, by extension, properties) are not objects and, thus, contrary to Russell, are to be regarded as in some sense unreal.

One obvious problem for this whole line of interpretation is that, in a previously cited remark in the *Notebooks,* Wittgenstein appears explicitly to deny this claim: "Relations and properties, etc. are *objects,* too" (NB 61). Similarly, in a conversation about the *Tractatus* in 1930–31, he is quoted as saying: " 'Objects' also include relations: a proposition is not two things connected by a relation. 'Thing' and 'relation' are on the same level. The objects hang as it were in a chain" (CL 120). Still, we need not conclude from this that 3.1432 is therefore an attempt to establish that relations and properties *are,* after all, constituents of the propositional fact.[6] Rather, I suggest that the whole attempt to view this remark as centrally concerned, one way or the other, with the question of the nature of Russellian relations misses the point. For, indeed, can we automatically assume that the *Tractatus'* notation is to be assimilated to Russell's – that Wittgenstein holds the "R" in "aRb" to represent the sort of thing designated by "is lying on" in a sentence like "The book is lying on the table"? Close consideration of this remark in conjunction with its predecessor would seem to suggest, in this context at least, that this is not the case.

3.1431 asks us to reflect on the spatial relationships between tables, books, and so on in a propositional sign composed of these elements.

It is these mutual spatial relationships that are said to "express the sense" of the proposition. So, if we take a book lying on a table as a depiction of a pencil lying on a chair, it is the book's position vis-à-vis the table that would express the sense of this picture-proposition; this sense, we can say, consists in a particular arrangement of pictorial elements against the background of space. The point, as in 2.15, is thus to bring out the self-sufficiency, as it were, of the picture's sense: we are to see it is just *that* the pictorial elements stand to each other in the particular way they do that allows the picture-proposition to be expressive, to depict some definite arrangement of objects in the world. Nothing further is involved – only the taking of these pictorial elements as a fact within space.

But it cannot always be literal physical space – or not this alone – that constitutes the background against which the elements in an arbitrary propositional sign aRb are able to depict, since not all pictures are spatial (as 2.182 makes clear).[7] Instead, as we have suggested, in moving to an explicit account of the proposition, we are involved in generalizing in a certain way the earlier remarks about the picture. It would seem, therefore, that as the expressiveness of the spatial picture takes place against the backdrop of a spatial form, the expressiveness or sense of the logical picture should be understood against the backdrop of the logical form. We can then ask: how are we now to understand, in general, the connection amongst the elements of the logical picture, the proposition? It is, I suggest, just this question, the question of the general nature of the propositional unity, not the issue of the reality or unreality of spatial, temporal, and other so-called material relations, which represents Wittgenstein's actual concern here.[8]

His response will then be seen to parallel – and provide a further elaboration of – his remarks about the structure of the picture at 2.14-2.15. We "must not say" that the complex sign "aRb" says "a stands in relation R to b," because to do so would lead us toward a confused understanding of the expressive power of the proposition. For in putting matters in this way, one seems to conceive of the proposition as essentially made up of a number of distinct elements that stand in need of unification. We are then naturally brought to focus on the apparent special relation reflected in the propositional sign, to see *it* as the key to the explanation of the proposition's ability to have a sense. Thus we become tempted to posit the existence of something like a "logical form" to hold together the propositional elements, as in Russell's multiple relation theory,[9] or to speak, as Frege does, of the inherent "unsaturatedness" of the function as making possible its combining with an object in the judgment.[10]

Wittgenstein seeks to eliminate these temptations at their root. To say along with the *Tractatus* "That 'a' stands in a certain relation to 'b' says that aRb," is not to replace one account of the nature of the propositional unity with another, but rather to *give up* the whole attempt to inquire into such a question. It is to see that the claim that, for example, the function sign is able to combine with a name *because* functions have some special connection with objects puts the cart before the horse; instead, we are acknowledging, it is only because these constituents do combine to yield a significant proposition that we are able to draw the distinction between functions and objects in the first place. Wittgenstein's point, then, is that our entire hold on the supposed relation between a and b in the assertion that aRb is parasitic on how we are able to operate with "a" and "b." We can thus say no more of the unity characterizing the significant proposition than that it consists in the particular *way* these elements hang together in the propositional sign.[11] The relation R, on this view, is then merely an internal feature of our notation, an outgrowth of the way *we* have decided to preserve the propositional unity in our analysis; it corresponds to what might also be expressed in the use of different signs for functions and objects, as when we write "f(a)."

All of this is summed up for Wittgenstein by saying that a proposition must be distinguished from a name, as he maintains in the remark following 3.1432: "States of affairs (*Sachlagen*) can be described but not *named.* (Names resemble points; propositions resemble arrows, they have sense)" (TLP 3.144). To suppose that a *Sachlage* could be named is inevitably to be led into searching for some further element, something that must be *added* to the proposition in order for it to be capable of expressing that fact. In seeing the proposition as akin to an arrow, by contrast, we are acknowledging the intimate connection between being a proposition and having a sense. An arrow does not connect to the direction it specifies by means of some intermediary; rather, it *is* the specification of a direction. Similarly, the sense of the proposition – its "direction" – cannot be viewed as external to the proposition's nature, but is instead constituitive of it: sensicality, we might say, is nothing other than the particular arrangement of propositional elements against the backdrop of logical space. Notice, however, that this whole account quite naturally opens up the question of the nature of this supposed "backdrop," the possibility of the proposition. Thus, just as Wittgenstein's discussion of the pictorial fact was seen to clear a space for an inquiry into the nature of the pictorial form, so here his inquiry turns to the nature of the logical form. And as that earlier account centered around the essential or nonarbitrary dimension of the pictorial element, so at this point he is concerned to investigate what is essential in the name.

III

The *Tractatus'* account of the name is bound up with the idea of a complete analysis of the proposition: "In propositions thoughts can be so expressed that to the objects of the thoughts correspond the elements of the propositional sign. These elements I call 'simple signs' (*einfache Zeichen*) and the proposition 'completely analyzed.' The simple signs employed in propositions are called names" (TLP 3.2–3.202). Among the many mysteries that the *Tractatus* presents, one has always concerned what an actual analysis into elementary propositions consisting only of names might look like; Wittgenstein notoriously never offers an example. That this omission is no mere accident on his part, but is instead a necessary consequence of his whole conception of logical analysis, should be evident from 5.5571 alone: "If I cannot give elementary propositions *a priori* then it must be obvious nonsense to try to give them."[12] Still, we may grant that it will be nonsense as far as Wittgenstein is concerned to give an example of a completely analyzed proposition, while still inquiring into why the *possibility* of such an analysis is thought to be so important. Through a consideration of this issue, we can gain an understanding of the *Tractatus'* view of the name and the nature of logical form.

The key to making sense of the *Tractatus'* position in this regard lies in a close consideration of 3.24, a remark that we began to discuss in the previous chapter.[13] Let us now quote this remark in its entirety:

> A proposition about a complex stands in internal relation to the proposition about its constituent part.
> A complex can only be given by its description, and this will either be right or wrong. The proposition in which there is mention of a complex, if this does not exist, becomes not nonsense but simply false.
> That a propositional element signifies a complex can be seen from an

> indeterminateness in the propositions in which it occurs. We *know* that everything is not yet determined by this proposition. (The notation for generality *contains* a prototype).
> The combination of the symbols of a complex in a simple symbol can be expressed by a definition.

In our earlier discussion of this passage, we suggested that part of Wittgenstein's concern here is to bring out the misleading nature of the notion of the complex. If our intuitive understanding of "complex" is of a term designating an entity having constituents or parts of some sort – and it is difficult to imagine what other sense could be given to this notion – then it would seem that any analysis of a proposition making mention of a complex would proceed by way of a further description. But, as we saw, Wittgenstein points out that this is just to say that whatever corresponds to the nonsimple propositional element is, from the point of view of logic, not a genuine component of the world, an object. Its complexity is not *named,* but is rather made manifest through another proposition, or series of propositions; structure is represented only by structure, as has been stressed in the picture theory.

In the first instance, then, reflection on the notion of analysis helps to make sharp the distinction just drawn at 3.144 between the name and the proposition. It now becomes clear that the components of the unanalyzed proposition should not be construed as names, simply by virtue of their superficial appearance as the designators of entities. At the same time, though, this account leads us to wonder about how ordinary language manages to function, to make contact with the simple objects corresponding to the genuine names. It may seem as if Wittgenstein is committing himself to the claim that the sense of the unanalyzed proposition is somehow undetermined, that we therefore have to wait on analysis, on logic to tell us what we really mean. Is such a view not implied in the above assertion that the appearance of the complex is marked by an "indeterminateness" in the proposition? Certainly Russell reads Wittgenstein in this way, suggesting in the Introduction that the *Tractatus* is concerned to lay down "conditions for a logically perfect language" and that ordinary language only has meaning "in proportion as it approaches to the ideal language which we postulate" (TLP, p. 8).

But Wittgenstein explicitly disavows this conception in the *Notebooks:* "This is surely clear: the propositions which are the only ones that humanity uses will have a sense just as they are and don't wait upon a future analysis to acquire a sense" (NB 62).[14] And, indeed, this same idea is expressed in the above passage from the *Tractatus.* For in saying that the proposition about the constituent (i.e., the analyzing proposition) is "internally" related to the proposition about the complex, Wittgenstein would seem to be calling attention to the way in which logical analysis demands the *preservation* of sense, the way in which analysis could not be possible unless this were the case. To illustrate, let us consider Russell's way of handling nondenoting concepts in his Theory of Descriptions (an important example, given that Wittgenstein here and at 4.0031 seems to regard it as the paradigm of analysis). Whatever we are to say about the correctness of Russell's treatment of sentences like "The present king of France is not bald," we must recognize that his suggested analysis can have a hope of admissibility only if we are willing to regard the analyzed expression – "$-\exists y\ (By\ \&\ \forall x\ (Px \leftrightarrow x=y))$" – as, in Quinean language, a *paraphrase* of at least some aspect of the unanalyzed. This whole enterprise would thus seem to depend on the original proposition already having what Wittgenstein at 3.23 and 3.251 calls a "determinate" (*Bestimmte*) sense.

On this account, a certain "indeterminateness" in the nonelementary proposition then serves as a means of allowing for the possibility of its analysis – which is to say for the possibility of the *definiteness* of its sense. This idea may seem to have an aura of paradox about it. But Wittgenstein's point becomes clearer when we understand the important claim in the above passage that we *know* that everything has not been determined by the unanalyzed proposition. The suggestion here would seem to be that the undeniable vagueness we find in the nonelementary proposition is in a certain sense circumscribed: just because I can take into account the way in which my expression is imprecise it is able to function perfectly adequately in ordinary contexts.

Wittgenstein elaborates this further in the *Notebooks:*

> If the complexity of an object is definitive of the sense of the proposition, then it must be portrayed in the proposition to the extent that it does determine the sense. . . . For if I am talking about, e.g., this watch, and mean something complex by that and nothing depends upon the way it is compounded, then a generalization will make its appearance in the

> proposition and the fundamental forms of the generalization will be completely determinate *so far as they are given at all* (NB 63–4).

Let us suppose that I assert that a watch is lying on the table and wish to infer from this that a wheel inside the watch is also lying on the table. "The watch" here can be said to refer to something complex, in that awareness of the referent's composition is necessary for fully understanding what I mean. But this is not to say that I must conduct a complete investigation into the physical makeup of the watch before I can speak meaningfully about it. Central to the *Tractatus* is the thought that sensicality must be conceived as independent of the way things happen to stand (see, e.g., TLP 4.061: "If one does not observe that propositions have a sense independent of the facts, one can easily believe that true and false are two relations between signs and things signified with equal rights."). My claim about the watch then *makes room* for that (apparent) object's complexity without committing itself, as it were, to a full specification of its components; it is enough for the sense of this proposition for me to know of the thing lying on the table simply that *there is* some mechanism inside of it. Definiteness of sense would thus appear to be compatible with, indeed made possible by, a certain indefiniteness in our ordinary propositions.

We can now see why both 3.24 and the *Notebooks* passage above speak of generality in connection with the nonelementary proposition. For the indeterminateness that marks the appearance of a complex is just the arbitrariness that, from Wittgenstein's perspective, is intrinsic to a generalization. The details of his view of generality will have to await our discussion of the quantifier in the next chapter, but the key idea is that "the watch" in the above nonelementary proposition is being treated in effect as a variable. We know that the features of the object fall within a specified range of possibilities, but it is an indifferent matter, as far as *this* proposition is concerned, as to precisely where; "the watch" plays the part of an arbitrary member of what Wittgenstein will call a series of forms.

The role of *analysis,* it would then seem, is to specify in some manner the particular members of that series, to individuate that which is indicated in the unanalyzed proposition only *en masse* (i.e., as the close of 3.24 suggests, as a combination of symbols linked to a simple symbol only via definition). 2.0201, the previously discussed counterpart to 3.24, describes the process as follows: "Every statement about complexes can be analyzed (*zerlegen*) into a statement about their constituent parts, and into those propositions which completely describe the complexes" (TLP 2.0201). This remark is, of course, quite opaque, even by Tractarian standards. But given the above noted importance of Russell's Theory of Descriptions to Wittgenstein's conception of analysis,[15] we may suppose that the first part of this claim is envisioning something along these Russellian lines. That is, the "statement about [the] constituent parts" of the complex would involve a claim asserting the obtaining of a series of conditions – namely, all the categories or forms that would be necessary to describe this structure. Thus, if the watch in the above example could be completely characterized in terms of a description of the color (C) and shape (S) of its parts,[16] then the analysis of the proposition asserting that the watch is lying on the table – assuming that the phrase "lying on the table" (L) could be understood as indicating a form – would begin with an existentially quantified statement of the form: "$\exists x(Cx\&Sx\&Lx)$." The analysis would then be concluded – the statement about the complex would be resolved into those propositions in which that complex is "completely described" – when we have produced a series of sentences in which the quantifier no longer appears. Logical analysis can thus serve to present, in an absolutely perspicuous form, the sense that belongs to the propositions of ordinary language.[17]

Still, it may well seem, on the basis of this account, that an analysis of this nature must ultimately involve a kind of empirical investigation. For how would we determine what are the ultimate components of the watch (and hence what needed to be described by our analyzing propositions) without opening up that watch and literally taking apart piece by piece its internal mechanism? If Tractarian analysis indeed does entail such a process, however, it begins to seem as if sense *can't* be construed as independent of circumstances in the world. After all, given that I have not engaged in the appropriate investigation of the watch, it would appear that I must remain ignorant of much that has in fact been left open by the unanalyzed proposition in which a representative for this object appears. Hence I cannot be supposed to *really* understand my assertion "The watch is lying on the table" – such an understanding could only be had by a watchmaker or perhaps a physicist. And this is to say that analysis would then seem to be required to reveal the actual sense of the proposition – contrary to what we have suggested. Is this not the view to which Wittgenstein is ultimately committed?

The *Notebooks* makes it quite apparent that this is not the case: "If, e.g., I say that this watch is not in the drawer, there is absolutely no need for it to FOLLOW LOGICALLY that a wheel which is in the watch is not in the drawer, for perhaps I had not the least knowledge that the wheel was in the watch, and hence could not have meant by 'this watch' the complex in which the wheel occurs" (NB 64–65). Similarly, he remarks several pages later: "It is clear that *I know* what I *mean* (*meine*) by the vague proposition" (NB 70). For Wittgenstein, it would seem, there can be no question of my attempting to mean something of which I am completely unaware.[18] Tractarian analysis must instead always be understood as analysis of *my* sense, not of some idealized or unattainable sense.[19] Its purpose will not be to eliminate the vagueness of the unanalyzed proposition, but rather to characterize that vagueness – or, better, to show that such vagueness poses no threat to the ability of the ordinary sentence to express. Thus Wittgenstein comments in the *Notebooks* that his whole concern could be described as one of "*justify[ing]* the vagueness of ordinary sentences" (NB 70, emphasis mine).

Intrinsic to Wittgenstein's approach, we might then say, is a distinction between the vagueness of a sentence and the determinateness of its sense. Here he would seem implicitly to be moving against Frege and a Fregean approach to analysis.[20] Frege famously holds that a proper scientific concept is one that must be capable of deciding for every object in the universe, whether or not it falls under that concept.[21] A concept that does not have "sharp boundaries" in this sense is thought to be entirely meaningless.[22] For Wittgenstein, though, this is confusing a requirement for a more consistent application of signs – which indeed is important for genuine science – with a condition of their *sense*. The point can be brought out through consideration of another passage in the *Notebooks:*

> I tell someone "The watch is lying on the table" and now he says: "Yes, but if the watch were in such-and-such a position would you still say it was lying on the table?" And I should become uncertain. This shews that I did not know what I meant by "lying" *in general.* If someone were to drive me into a corner in this way in order to shew that I did not know what I meant, I should say: "I know what I mean; I mean just

> THIS," pointing to the appropriate complex with my finger. And in this complex I do actually have the two objects in a relation. (NB 70)

It is here admitted that I will not ordinarily be prepared to say of *all* possible locations of the watch whether or not it can be said to be lying on the table. But why should this be taken to imply that I did not know what I meant in the first place? It is not as if, in uttering my sentence, I am attempting to perform a scientific experiment and it is crucial to have something to say in every borderline case. Wittgenstein suggests instead that what is necessary for my proposition to have a determinate sense is only that it allows for *some* range of locations that will count as the watch's lying on the table (and some range that will count as its not doing so); for there to be something that I mean in this instance the existence of a paradigm case is sufficient. Surely, though, this condition is satisfied by the sentence about the watch, and, moreover, in its general formulation, by any sentence we should ordinarily count as meaningful. But then, on this account, *all* sense would turn out to be determinate sense – which is really to say that the notion of an intrinsic vagueness to what I *mean* must be seen as incoherent.[23]

We can now begin to see more clearly the idea behind Wittgenstein's demand that analysis be final or complete, as at 3.25: "There is one and only one complete analysis of the proposition." For, as 3.23 suggests, such an analysis would seem to represent nothing but a way of *expressing* the determinateness that characterizes the sense of the proposition: "The postulate of the possibility of the simple signs *is* the postulate of the determinateness of sense" (emphasis mine). The point, in other words, is this. If I mean anything at all by my utterance, I should be able to render this in a perspicuous form, in the manner discussed above (that is, through a description of all the logically relevant features of the elements in my proposition). The question then arises as to whether such a specification would be complete. To answer in the negative would seem to involve imagining that my assertion leaves something open intrinsically – as if I might later come to *discover* what I had originally meant. Witttgenstein's assertion of the determinateness of sense is then really equivalent to (what we have seen to be) his dismissal of such a possibility as nonsense.[24] Logical analysis must in principle always be completable.

It is thus evident that the *Tractatus'* principle of a complete analysis cannot be taken as a self-standing thesis about the nature of language but, rather, is to be understood as a way of undermining the supposition of an essential indeterminacy in the sense of a sentence. At the same time, however, reflecting on this idea brings into sharper relief the proper aim of a philosophical inquiry. For what would it mean to give a complete analysis in the Tractarian sense? Analysis, as we have seen, is a process of laying out in a perspicuous form exactly what I mean in uttering some particular sentence. It is, we might therefore say, a matter of bringing to light the *definitions* implicit in the seemingly simple signs of the nonelementary proposition, since 3.261 (in a manner similar to 3.24) holds: "Every defined sign signifies *via* those signs by which it is defined, and the definitions show the way" (TLP 3.261). This process of analysis will terminate when I have arrived at "primitive signs" (*Urzeichen*) that "cannot be analyzed further by any definition" (TLP 3.26) – that is to say when I have a sentence containing only genuine *names.* With the name we thus would appear to have a sign that can be given no further explanation of *how* it signifies; it is in some sense in immediate contact with the world.[25] In specifying the real names, it seems we are then making transparent the inner possibilities common to the world and the sentences that depict it, the logical core of reality. And that suggests that a complete analysis of the proposition will reveal nothing other than, on the one hand, the linguistic analogue to the pictorial form (the logical form), on the other, the timeless, unchanging substance described at the opening of the *Tractatus.*

The conditions that must be satisfied for a specification of substance can now be given more precise articulation: what is required is the identification of the referents or meanings (*Bedeutungen*) of the names in the fully analyzed proposition. Such a specification would, it seems, bring us almost literally to *see* the determinateness, the logical elements, that lie at the base of the significant proposition. Wittgenstein implies something of this sort in this passage from the *Prototractatus:*

> Although every word has meaning (*bedeutet*) via its definitions, this only means that these definitions are necessary in order to present in our sign-language the full linguistic depiction of the thought to whose expression the word contributes. But the definitions can be left tacit and the word does not then lose its meaning (*seine Bedeutung*), since it still stands in the same relation to the objects which are depicted by means of the definitions – only we do not specifically depict that relation. Naturally this often simplifies the sign-language and makes the

> understanding of it more and more difficult, because the decisive factor now lies outside the signs in something that is not expressed – their relation to their objects. (PT 3.202111)

A sharp contrast is here drawn between the purposes of logical analysis and those of ordinary human communication. While ordinary communication requires a certain simplicity of expression, logic seeks to articulate the full complexity of our language. Its aim in doing so is not to provide the elements of the proposition with a *Bedeutung* – as we have seen Wittgenstein's fundamental thought is that logical analysis cannot serve to "improve" our language in this way – but, rather, to lay bare the *relation* of the sign to that *Bedeutung*. The question of how the realization of this "decisive factor" is achieved by analysis then becomes the question addressed by the 3.3s.

IV

Still, it is not at once apparent just why there *is* a question here. For if the *Bedeutung* is the object for which the name stands, as 3.203 appears to state, and I have analyzed the proposition into names, what more is there for me to say about that *Bedeutung?* If you ask me who is in the room, and I tell you John, Mary, and Ivan, surely that reply would count as sufficient (even if it were incorrect). We might then suppose that Wittgenstein's ultimate point about the unsatisfiability of the logico-philosophical inquiry must depend on his later claim about the impossibility of specifying the elementary propositions *a priori* – as if that inquiry's goal would be realizable but for an unfortunate restriction on human analytical capacities.[26] But I suggest that this is not how his argument proceeds. Instead, the point of the upcoming remarks is precisely to see why the attempt to specify the *Bedeutungen* is *unlike* my above example of listing the individuals in a room by name. Wittgenstein's aim here, in other words, is to bring to the fore the essential ambiguity of the notion of a "logical object" – the very notion that lies at the heart of the thought of Frege and Russell.

Indeed, 3.3 has a distinctly Fregean ring to it, calling to mind his famous "context principle" from the *Foundations of Arithmetic.* "Only the proposition has sense; only in the context of a proposition has a name meaning" (TLP 3.3). We might suppose that Wittgenstein is here merely echoing what Ricketts has called Frege's "judgment-centered metaphysics."[27] But while it is true that Wittgenstein is emphasizing the primacy of the judgment, his way of developing this idea will assume a very un-Fregean cast. For what is the force of restricting the *Bedeutung* of the name to the propositional context? Wittgenstein's answer is developed through the new notion of an expression (*Ausdruck*). "Every part of a proposition which characterizes its sense I call an expression (a symbol). (The proposition itself is an expression). Expressions are everything – essential for the sense of the proposition – that propositions can have in common with one another. An expression characterizes a form and a content" (TLP 3.31). An expression is any part of a proposition that contributes to the sense of the whole. We can then only identify expressions by reference to the propositions in which they occur; it is incoherent to suppose that they might occur in isolation. (The limiting case of this claim will be the one in which the expression is a proposition.) That, however, is not to suggest that an expression is some sort of free-floating object that propositionally bound signs can alone latch on to successfully. Rather, the point is that an expression is *constituted* by the occurrence of some sign or signs within a certain set of propositions. It is, as 3.326 suggests, nothing but the sign in its "significant use."

To grasp an expression will then entail the recognition of a "common characteristic mark of a class of propositions" (TLP 3.311). Its appropriate presentation is by means of a variable in Wittgenstein's sense, which is, on the face of it, a Russellian propositional function "whose values are the propositions which contain the expression" (TLP 3313). Thus, for example, one expression would be given by seeing what is common to the propositions "The cup is red," "The book is red," "The table is red," and so on – that is to say by the propositional function "x is red." Now it is important to emphasize here that the mere occurrence of the words "is red" does not by itself ensure that these sentences have something in common; again we must pay attention to the *way* these signs contribute to the sense of the propositions in which they occur. Wittgenstein repeats this point several times, for example, at 3.323: "In the proposition 'Green is green' – where the first word is a proper name and the last an adjective – these words have not merely different meanings but they are *different symbols* [expressions]." Similarly, although less obviously, he suggests in a later conversation with Schlick, Waismann, and Carnap that in the sentences "The table is brown" and "The surface of the table is brown" the phrase "is brown" constitutes two different expressions. After all, while in the first sentence "is heavy" can be meaningfully substituted for "is brown," in the second this yields nonsense.[28] An expression can be given only through a consideration of *all* the propositions in which some set of signs can occur.

Now we can begin to become clearer on the import of Wittgenstein's "context principle," which is restated in a somewhat different form at 3.314: "An expression only has meaning (*Bedeutung*) in a proposition. Every variable can be conceived as a propositional variable." The context principle would seem to be somehow equivalent to, or explained by, the claim identifying all variables as propositional variables. This latter identification may at first seem surprising, as if Wittgenstein were denying the possibility of the predicate calculus. Clearly, however, such cannot be his intent. This remark must instead be understood as a way of making evident what is meant by "the context" in which the *Bedeutung* of an expression is to be considered. The proper presentation of an expression is, as we have seen, by way of a variable. 3.314 is then emphasizing how the introduction of the variable requires our already being *given* a class of propositions, how the variable serves only as a kind of description of what those propositions share logically. This indeed is stated more or less explicitly at 3.316: "What values the variable can assume is determined. The determinations of the values *is* the variable." We might say that the variable is ultimately nothing but a certain way of regarding a sign or sequence of signs; it is the sign seen *as* logical mark of a class of propositions.[29] Wittgenstein's context principle then serves essentially to equate this logical dimension of the sign with the *Bedeutung* of the expression. We understand a meaning only when we look to *how* the propositional sign functions within a whole class of propositions.

With this idea in mind, we can make sense of Wittgenstein's way of introducing the notion of *Bedeutung* at 3.203: "The name means (*bedeutet*) the object. The object is its meaning (*Bedeutung*). ("A" is the same sign as "A.")" The natural inclination – one that is followed by most Tractarian commentators – is to suppose that Wittgenstein is here suggesting that "object" and "meaning" are simply interchangeable, and that the name therefore stands for a meaning in the same way that a red patch might serve as a pictorial representative of a chair. But we saw earlier in our discussion of the picture theory that the *Tractatus* uses the term *vertreten* to designate this arbitrary relation between a pictorial element and an object.[30] And indeed this same term appears again at 3.22: "In the proposition the name is the representative of (*vertritt*) an object." It appears, then, that the *bedeuten* relation has to do not with the arbitrary aspect of the relation between a sign and its referent, but, rather, with what Wittgenstein would call an "essential" feature – namely, the *way* the sign contributes to the sense of the proposition in which it occurs. It is to stress how grasping this nonarbitrary dimension of the name entails considering its occurrence in a whole class of propositions that Wittgenstein adds the parenthetical remark about "A" being the same sign as "A."[31] Just as in the first part of the picture theory, then, we see that two dimensions of the relation between signs and reality are distinguished – and, correspondingly, just as in our discussion of the text's opening remarks, that two dimensions of the objects thereby depicted also emerge. (Note how 3.31's reference to an expression characterizing a "form and content" echoes 2.025's similar claim about substance.) What the name "means" is thus indeed the object, but the object considered only with respect to its form.

It now becomes clearer why the identification of the *Bedeutung* will be of central importance in the *Tractatus* and, moreover, how such a task is tied in to the Fregean and Russellian projects. For if the meanings of the names are equated with the forms of objects, then, given what we have said about the latter notion in the previous chapter, in specifying those meanings we will have specified the fundamental categories of thought or language – that is to say, the logical forms. The endeavor to make evident such categories would seem to be what Russell has in mind in the *Principles of Mathematics* when he speaks of the need for gaining a clear grasp of the "indefinables," a task he presents as "the chief part of philosophical logic."[32] In Frege's thought, too, the concern with the fundamental logical categories is central, expressing itself in his distinction between functions and objects. But, then, given the connection between a specification of the meanings of the primitive signs and the more grandly metaphysical aims inherent in the remarks of the 1s and 2s, it would seem that Wittgenstein is here bringing out the truly exalted nature of the Fregean and Russellian projects. That is, if the attempt to identify our basic logical categories is really another way of getting at the fundamental connection between language and the world, the unchanging substance that is somehow at the heart of both, then Wittgenstein would be showing that the work of these authors has even greater import than they might have imagined. The *Tractatus* could then rightly be said to be completing that work, bringing it to its inevitable conclusion.

Of course, we have already seen in our discussion of the first part of the picture theory that Wittgenstein's "completion" of (what he takes to be) the Frege/Russell project will entail a complete shift in our understanding of its nature. And, indeed, just such a shift begins to become evident in this context in the remarks concerning Russell's theory of types. "From this observation [about the nature of logical syntax] we get a further view – into Russell's *Theory of Types*. Russell's error is shown by the fact that in drawing up his symbolic rules he has to speak about the meaning of the signs" (TLP 3.331). The theory of types is, of course, Russell's attempt to avoid the class paradox – the contradiction that ensues from assuming the class of all classes that do not contain themselves as members – and its analogues. In essence, it involves supposing a hierarchy of logical types of entities: at the bottom level individuals, then (according to the presentation in *Principia Mathematica*) propositional functions that apply to individuals, then propositional functions that apply to propositional functions that apply to individuals, and so on. The theory of types serves to restrict the application of the propositional function only to entities of the immediately preceding level and thereby allows us to avoid the paradoxes.

Still, while the above remark makes it clear that the *Tractatus* regards this approach as somehow illegitimate, it is not at once obvious just what sort of "error" Russell is thought to have committed. Many commentators suppose that Wittgenstein's criticism is made in light of a proposed technical alternative to the theory of types, one in which no mention is made of the referents of the signs.[33] Certainly, the allusion to "logical syntax" could well seem to support the view of the *Tractatus* as arguing for a Hilbert-style, purely syntactical approach to logic:[34] "In logical syntax the meaning (*Bedeutung*) of a sign ought never to play a role; it must admit of being established without mention being thereby made of the *meaning* of a sign; it ought to presuppose *only* the description of the expressions" (TLP 3.33). Nonetheless, even without an understanding of the role of the term *Bedeutung* in the *Tractatus*, it should be evident from the reference here to the primacy of "description" of expressions that this passage, rather than constituting some new departure on Wittgenstein's part, is simply a continuation of the above discussion of the variable, of the idea of analysis more generally. And that suggests that we should not view his talk of "logical syntax" as part of an attempt to advocate some particular technical approach to the study of logic, any more than we can suppose him to have provided specific guidelines as to how to carry out a complete analysis.[35] Instead, it would seem that Wittgenstein is here and throughout concerned only to get us to reflect on the *idea* of analysis, on how in general an analysis is to be carried out. Such reflection, as we shall see, is meant to reveal not a slight defect in the Russellian approach to logic, but rather a fundamental confusion at its heart.

I suggest, then, that the real nature of the *Tractatus'* criticism of Russell becomes clear when we view it in light of the above discussion of the context principle.[36] For what is the theory of types ultimately seeking to accomplish? From Wittgenstein's perspective, it must be understood as part of the attempt to complete the kind of analysis spoken of in the *Tractatus* – that is, as an effort to set forth the fundamental logical categories. Russell is seen as claiming that, by drawing the distinctions between individuals and propositional functions and between the different levels of propositional functions, he has specified the logical forms underlying all thought and language. In then suggesting that Russell must "speak about the meaning of the signs," Wittgenstein is really saying that the theory of types is committed to treating the logical forms as if they might be named – that is, as if they constituted further constituents of the fact that could be specified in advance. Now, to hold that this move is an error is not to seek to impose some restriction on what such a theory can meaningfully express – a meta-theory of types as it were.[37] Rather, what Wittgenstein is trying to bring out is how this involves a misconstrual of what it would mean to complete the task of analysis; we are supposed to recognize that the referent of a name *couldn't* be what we are looking for as the endpoint of our inquiry. After all, we have just seen that to arrive at the *Bedeutung* of an expression one must consider a whole class of propositions with regard to what they have in common and determine how that common element contributes to the sense of these propositions. One might then take a sentence like "The book is red" as characterizing an expression (recall from 3.31 that the proposition itself is an expression), but only when some subset of these signs is viewed in terms of its role in a particular class of propositions does it give us a meaning. Again, a form is determined only by viewing some string of signs *as* a logical mark.

For Russell, though, it is almost the opposite. With the theory of types, he seems to be imagining that our grasp on the significant sentence comes by way of a prior hold on the form. To believe that we could *say* that, for example, propositional functions ranging over individuals constitute one logical type would appear to involve supposing that it is this variable that dictates to the propositions constituting its domain – as if the logical form might represent a criterion of sense. For Wittgenstein, Russell's need to speak of what his signs mean bespeaks a tendency to attribute to logic just the wrong kind of priority.

Indeed, we might say that Russell's belief that there is even a *need* for a theory of types is, from the Tractarian perspective, already an indication of a fundamental confusion. This is what is suggested in 3.333:

> A function cannot be its own argument, because the functional sign already contains the prototype of its own argument and it cannot contain itself. If, for example, we suppose that the function *F(fx)* could be its own argument, then there would be a proposition *"F(F (fx))"* and in this the outer function *F* and the inner function *F* must have different meanings (*Bedeutungen*); for the inner has the form $\phi(fx)$, the outer the form $\psi(\phi(fx))$. Common to both functions is only the letter *"F,"* which by itself signifies nothing. This is at once clear, if instead of *"F(F(u))"* we write *"*$(\exists\phi) : F(\phi u) . \phi u = Fu$.*"* Herewith Russell's paradox vanishes.

Wittgenstein's point is that when we become clear on what it means to treat a function sign as a variable rather than as a name, we recognize that, in a sense, there *is* no paradox with which to concern ourselves. "F" here is a schematic rendering of a class of propositions of a particular form; the meaning of "F" will then be determined by the use of certain signs common to that class. In "F(F(fx))," the first "F" and the second will therefore not have the same meaning, since, to use Russellian terminology, the first "F" ranges over propositional functions of type *n*, while the second ranges over functions of type $n + 1$.[38] The idea, in other words, is that the function (i.e., the variable) is constituted entirely by the logical role it plays and these functions play different roles, given the differences in the classes of propositions that they characterize. But then that is to say that it will be *impossible* to construct a (significant) expression of the form F(F), where the two "Fs" constitute the same type of propositional function. This is, of course, just the restriction that the theory of types is trying to institute, but Wittgenstein wants to show how this restriction is there expressed in a misleading way. For it is not, as the theory of types would suggest, *because* the two "Fs" in F(Fx) are of the same type that this expression yields nonsense. Rather, it is just because the expression yields nonsense that we say these "F's" are of the same type. One is reminded here of 3.1432 ("We must not say, 'The complex sign "aRb" says "a stands in relation R to b' "; but we must say, '*That* "a" stands in a certain relation to "b" says *that aRb*'."): Wittgenstein's aim is once more to bring out how our hold on a notion of logical form is parasitic on how we speak, on what it makes sense to say. To recognize this is to acknowledge that a *theory* of types is unnecessary, if by that we are imagining some *a priori* restriction on what is permissible logically. Rather than seeking to "solve" "a paradox," our focus instead should be on gaining a clear understanding of the workings of our language. With such an understanding, we will be no more tempted to speak of "the class of all classes that are not self-members" than we would to ask about the weight of a noise.[39] Thus Wittgenstein adds at 3.334: "The rules of logical syntax must follow of themselves, if we only know how every single sign signifies" (TLP 3.334).

V

But if it is now more apparent why the theory of types is dismissed as misleading, we still have to become clearer on the nature of the alternative being proposed by the *Tractatus*. How will the meaning of a sign or set of signs be expressed in what Wittgenstein would consider an appropriately constructed language? From the above discussion, it is certainly evident that such a language will not include any *names* for *Bedeutungen*; that, however, does not alone tell us how a Tractarian analysis of a proposition is to proceed. Let us then use as our example "The watch is lying on the table." In our analysis, as we have seen, we will be concerned to make perspicuous what is needed for this proposition to express its sense. In this case, what will be required is, say, a color dimension, as well as a position dimension. A thorough characterization of what I mean by "watch" and "lying on the table" will, of course, require other dimensions as well, the full enumeration of which will only be given with the completion of the analysis. But suppose that color and spatial position are in fact among the dimensions, the forms that will be needed in the complete analysis; these, in other words, are two of the *meanings* involved in the above sentence expressing its sense.[40] Suppose, further, that I choose to express the analyzed sentence by means of a coordinate system (Wittgenstein in fact speaks of such a system at TLP 3.41 and in a number of places in the *Notebooks*[41]): one set of x- and y-axes will be marked off in units of measurement, another set of axes perhaps in units of color and brightness. I will then express the claim that some position on the table has some particular shade of color as, for example, the ordered pair <3,2> conjoined with an ordered pair representing a location on the color/brightness scales.

Now what is central to notice here is that this specification makes no mention of *either* position or color – the names in this language refer only to specific points within the coordinate system. And, indeed, as long as the scale of my coordinate system is well chosen initially I will be able to describe the color of *any* position on the surface of the table in the same manner, simply checking off, as it were, the appropriate points on my scale. The forms of color and spatial position are thus absorbed into my method of representation; they become part of the means by which I can describe the world rather than further elements that themselves have linguistic representatives. In the complete analysis of the above sentence, *all Bedeutungen* will similarly vanish into the particular system in terms of which reality is to be depicted.

Reflection on the notion of analysis thus makes evident how I might give a thorough description of the world without ever needing to have names of meanings, of logical forms. One is naturally reminded here of Frege's aforementioned concept "horse" problem[42] and his idea that the "ordinary language" distinction between concepts and objects will ultimately express itself only in the use of the signs of a canonical notation. Still, if Wittgenstein is simply following and extending Frege's insight,[43] then the objection that we might bring against the latter also would seem applicable to the *Tractatus*. For one might want to ask Frege just why his Begriffsschrift is supposed to be criterial with regard to the concept "horse" problem. Why does the fact that the Fregean concept-script does not allow us to treat concepts as objects show that it is a "confusion" to attempt to make this equation in ordinary language, as Benno Kerry does? In the same way, then, one could seemingly ask Wittgenstein why the possibility of a certain kind of analysis demonstrates that *Bedeutungen* "really" cannot be named. Indeed, we seemingly *have* to speak of the logical forms in initially setting up the coordinate systems. For what reason are we to dismiss such talk as "nonsense"?

These objections fail to take into account the dialectical nature of the *Tractatus;* we might say, then, that they serve only to bring out the *difference* between Wittgenstein's thought and Frege's.[44] For Wittgenstein, far from being committed to supposing that the analyzed sentence constitutes the "correct" form of expression, is in fact concerned to suggest the *nonsensicality* of such a notion. His whole position in the *Tractatus* (and in the later philosophy as well) rests on the assumption that we can make perfect sense with the language we already have: analysis, as we have suggested, is discussed not in order to correct supposed deficiencies in our ability to speak and communicate, but rather only for the purpose of making clear the nature of the logical investigation itself. As far as Wittgenstein is concerned, then, we can in "colloquial language" speak of "color," "spatial position," and so on, or refrain from doing so – nothing whatsoever is here at stake. It is only if our aim is to identify the fundamental logical categories of our language (i.e., if we are engaged in philosophy) that his distinctions between what can be spoken of and what cannot come into play.[45] In this case, then, in reflecting on the absorption of the logical forms into the particular coordinate systems that we set up, what we are meant to see is how everything we (as philosophers) would properly be looking for is built into the *way* we will speak. And that is just to say that it must be nonsense to seek to specify the object of our search in advance (and remember that for Wittgenstein it is only in such an *a priori* manner that a logico-philosophical inquiry is to be conducted). For although the specification of some position in, say, color space only makes sense against the background of a particular coordinate system, that coordinate system itself is *defined* by the range of significant "color propositions." This becomes particularly evident when we reflect on how we would determine whether or not such a system is adequate. Wittgenstein will later say that it is a matter of the set of signs having the right "logical/mathematical multiplicity" (see 4.04–4.0411, 5.475), but that simply means that it allows us to express all and only what we want to express – that is, that with this system we never expect to end up either at a loss for words, as it were, or depicting an impossible state of affairs.[46] Notice, however, that, were either such eventuality to take place, we would reject this representational system (and not our ordinary standards of intelligibility) as inadequate.[47] Criterial in logical analysis is what we can meaningfully say and it is on this that we necessarily remain dependent.[48]

Wittgenstein's whole point here is then really summed up at 3.327: "The sign determines a logical form only together with its logical-syntactical application." It is, in other words, through the significant *use* of the propositional sign alone that the logical form, the *Bedeutung* of an expression will emerge.[49] This, in turn, brings us back to the central point of the picture theory. For this notion of the emergence of the logical form through the proposition's application mirrors precisely the way we have seen the *pictorial* form, the inner possibilities common to the picture and reality, to be structured through the projection of the picture on to reality. And just as this latter idea led Wittgenstein to hold that the pictorial form can only be shown, so we see here a clear anticipation of 4.121: "Propositions cannot represent the logical form: this mirrors itself in the propositions. That which mirrors itself in language, language cannot represent. That which expresses *itself* in language, *we* cannot express by language. The propositions show the logical form of reality. They exhibit it." This remark, together with Wittgenstein's subsequent insistence that that which "*can* be shown *cannot* be said" (TLP 4.1212), is standardly taken as one of the clearest indications that the *Tractatus* is committed to the supposition of deep, but inexpressible features of reality. But our discussion of the 3s should make plain how this interpretation of the show/say distinction is no more appropriate here than in the context of the picture theory. For instead of flatly asserting the existence of an ineffable domain of form, Wittgenstein is to be regarded as again attempting to make evident the nature of the logico-philosophical inquiry itself. To hold that logical form is only shown is to emphasize how the whole of the philosopher's apparent subject matter is inextricably built into the coordinate system that allows us to express, that it makes no sense to *look for* it. A complete analysis into elementary propositions consisting only of names will make perspicuous how this is the case, not by allowing us to "better understand" logical form (whatever that would mean), but by removing the temptation to imagine that there is anything to be understood in the first place.

This point about the inherent unsatisfiablility of the philosophical endeavor is further brought out at 3.3421:

> A particular method of symbolizing may be unimportant, but it is always important that this is a *possible* method of symbolizing. And this happens as a rule in philosophy: The single thing proves over and over again to be unimportant, but the possibility of every single thing reveals something about the nature of the world. (TLP 3.3421)

Here Wittgenstein is asking us to reflect on what it means to seek a logical or philosophical *result.* It seems to go almost without saying that a logical inquiry can terminate only when it has seized on the correct formulation of its subject matter, when it has in some sense captured the object of its search. This assumption finds expression in Frege's very need to construct his Begriffsschrift, the presumed canonical presentation of the logic of our language. Wittgenstein's claim that it is only the *possibility* of a particular symbolism that reveals something about the essence of the world is then meant to emphasize the emptiness of the attempt to specify that essence. For if, as he has suggested, the logical dimension of the sign of any language only emerges in the way that sign is applied, that aspect must be, so to speak, spread out across a class of propositions: logic is not located at some single point in a system of signs, but is made manifest by the language as a whole. There is then in a sense nothing for us to *do* to specify a logical form, nothing but to pay attention to the way the sign functions in the (significant) sentences in which it figures.

This of course does not preclude the attempt to develop a special notation, nor even deny that doing so might be helpful in certain ways. As Wittgenstein puts it:

> We can, for example, express what is common to all notations for the truth functions as follows: It is common to them that they all, for example, *can be replaced* by the notations of *"$-p$"* ("not *p*") and *"pvq"* ("*p* or *q*"). (Herewith is indicated the way in which a special possible notation can give us general information). (TLP 3.3441)

Certainly, then, it is permissible, as far as Wittgenstein is concerned, to use what is in this case Russellian notation for the truth functions.

But to say that this is a "possible notation" or that this constitutes a mode of expression which might "replace" other means of expressing the truth functions is to suggest that the notation does not *give us* by itself the inner logic of our language. In order to see the Russellian truth functional notation as revealing something of the "essence" of the world we must take these signs together with all other notations that can express the same sense. We must, in other words, see these signs as characterizing an *expression* in the Tractarian sense of the term. But that makes evident that there is nothing logically privileged about the Russellian notation, that these signs stand on the same level as any other in the class that they serve to characterize.

Again, then, it becomes apparent how the inquiry into the logical forms turns back on itself: what begins as an attempt to specify the necessary features of the world ends with the recognition that these extend as far as our language itself, that the "specification" can be no more than an acknowledgment that we speak, sometimes with sense, sometimes nonsensically. This is just the thrust of 3.341 and 3.3411, which might be taken as the culmination of the discussion of the 3s. After drawing the distinction between accidental and essential features of the proposition, Wittgenstein states:

> The essential in a proposition is therefore that which is common to all propositions which can express the same sense. And in the same way in general the essential in a symbol is that which all symbols which can fulfill the same purpose have in common. One could therefore say the real name is that which all symbols, which signify an object, have in common. It would then follow, step by step, that no sort of composition was essential for a name. (TLP 3.341 and 3.3411)

This notion of the "essential" in a symbol or expression is just another way of speaking of its *Bedeutung.* To hold that this essential aspect is arrived at by seeing what all symbols that can fulfill the same purpose have in common is thus really to reiterate how the logical form is spread out across a whole class of propositions. But then that is to suggest that the "real name" that logic seeks is ultimately no name at all: its "composition" disintegrates precisely because what it refers to is not a *thing,* in any ordinary sense of the term but an internal feature of our own language.

This in turn brings out more fully the inherent ambiguity of the notion at the center of the whole logico-philosophical inquiry, the notion of a logical object.[50] It is not that Wittgenstein wishes to flatly deny the existence of such entities, to hold that they are pure fictions. His aim instead is to get us to see how their "existence" rests on the existence of objects as the arbitrary (or accidental) referents of names in the sensical proposition. The logical object is not a thing, but, we might say, a *way* of regarding the components of our genuine propositions; it is the propositional constituent viewed in a special light. This section of the *Tractatus* intends to show precisely the fragility of such a perspective.

VI

Given this way of understanding the discussion of analysis in the 3s, Wittgenstein's blunt characterization of the notion of an object as a "pseudo-concept" at 4.1272 should come as no surprise. Indeed, it quickly becomes apparent how the distinction between formal concepts/properties/relations and proper concepts/properties/relations is really a kind of paraphrase of the points that have emerged in the passages we have been considering. Thus, we find first at 4.122: "We can speak in a certain sense of formal properties of objects and atomic facts, or of properties of the structures of facts, and in the same sense of formal relations and relations of structures." In *what* sense can we speak of such formal properties and relations? Wittgenstein makes clear in 4.122 that the term "internal" can be substituted for "formal" in these contexts. An internal property, however, is one that "it is unthinkable that its object . . . not possess" (TLP 4.123): two shades of blue, for example, stand in the internal relation of brighter and darker in that standing in that relation is constitutive of what they are; to remove these "objects" from that relation is "unthinkable" just because we can have no independent handle on their identity.[51] But then it would seem that we can "speak of" formal properties and relations only in the sense that we can utter propositions in which they figure as internal features. Thus, we might say that white should be added to that magenta paint if the latter is to approach sky blue or remark on how, at sunset, the sky has deepened to become magenta. By contrast, we (assuming we were fluent speakers of English) would not remark on the magenta color of the sunset and then go on to wonder if the sky were darker than its ordinary color. That magenta is darker than sky blue is, it would seem, *built into* the statements in which these words can meaningfully occur – which is to say that what we would want to express by this string of signs is shown by the existence of a certain class of propositions.

This in fact is what Wittgenstein proceeds to assert about internal properties and relations generally: "The holding of such internal properties and relations cannot, however, be asserted by propositions, but it shows itself in the propositions which represent the facts and treat of the objects in question" (TLP 4.122). We can then say, to use the terms of our above discussion, that the internal or formal features of a concept like "magenta" is properly presented by a propositional variable (or, perhaps, a number of propositional variables), whose values define the meaning of this notion. An expression like "magenta is darker than sky blue" will be absent from the resulting class – will be nonsense – just because it attempts, we might say, to *assert* a variable; it supposes that what is common to a number of propositions exists alongside those propositions, as a further fact to be represented. In attempting to state a formal relation or property, it is thus as if we were imagining that a triangle formed from the intersection of three lines might somehow be viewed apart from these (mere contingent) borders. Wittgenstein's purpose would then be to expose the incoherence of this fantasy of getting at the triangle itself, to get us to see that everything we are really after here emerges simply through a description of the boundary lines that characterize this figure.

Wittgenstein's remarks about "formal concepts" express much the same point:

> In the sense in which we speak of formal properties we can now speak also of formal concepts. . . . That anything falls under a formal concept as an object belonging to it, cannot be expressed by a proposition. But it is shown in the symbol for the object itself. (The name shows that it signifies an object, the numerical sign that it signifies a number, etc.) Formal concepts cannot, like proper concepts, be represented by a function. For their characteristics, the formal properties, are not expressed by the functions. The expression of a formal property is a feature (*Zug*) of certain symbols. The sign that signifies the characteristics of a formal concept is, therefore, a characterisic feature of all symbols, whose meanings fall under the concept. The expression of the formal concept is therefore a propositional variable in which only this characteristic feature is constant. (TLP 4.126)

We must first notice the position that the formal concept occupies within the overall Tractarian framework. Wittgenstein says that such a concept is a feature of certain symbols – that is, an expression of what these symbols have in common. But recall that the symbol (expression) is *itself* a way of characterizing a form, that which is common to a class of propositions. In speaking of a formal concept Wittgenstein has thus ascended a level from his earlier talk of the propositiotional variable; the proper means of expressing a formal concept will then presumably be through what he calls a "formal series" – that is, a whole system of symbols (such as the one characterizing the concept of being a successor) "ordered by internal relations" (TLP 4.1252). Nonetheless, Wittgenstein suggests that a formal concept is, just like an expression or symbol, presented by way of a propositional variable. He can then be said to recognize in this sense no type distinctions with regard to variables: the formal concept is spoken of in exactly the same terms as the expressions it serves to characterize.[52] (For this reason Wittgenstein asserts at 4.1271: "Every variable is the sign of a formal concept.") By contrast, though, there remains an essential difference between the propositional variable and its values. Thus, Wittgenstein suggests that the formal concept, as part of what some number of symbols *are,* cannot (meaningfully) be set down alongside the propositions that this concept ultimately serves to characterize, as if they all stood on the same level. Or, to shift to the previous metaphor, we could say that a formal concept like "object" must be conceived as part of the coordinate system that allows us to express, rather than constituting some determinate position within that framework. It will then be nonsense to attempt to make assertions about such notions.

4.1272, the first bald assertion of the nonsensicality of the central notions of Russellian and Fregean logic[53] – as well as those that the *Tractatus* itself has relied on – thus follows quite naturally from the previous remarks:

> So the variable name "x" is the proper sign of the pseudo-concept *object.* Wherever the word "object" ("thing," "entity," etc.) is rightly used, it is expressed in logical symbolism by the variable name. For example in the proposition "there are two objects which . . ." by "(∃x, y) . . .". Wherever it is used otherwise, i.e., as a proper concept word, there arise

> nonsensical (*unsinnige*) pseudo-propositions. So one cannot, e.g., say "There are objects" as one says "There are books." Nor "There are 100 objects" or "There are χ_0 objects." The same holds of the words "Complex," "Fact," "Function," "Number," etc. They all signify formal concepts and are presented in logical symbolism by variables, not by functions or classes (as Frege and Russell thought). Expressions like "1 is a number," "there is only one number nought," and all like them are nonsensical. (It is as nonsensical to say "there is only one 1" as it would be to say: 2 + 2 is at 3 o'clock equal to 4).

"Object," "fact," "function," "complex," "number," and so on are all formal concepts in the above sense and consequently will not figure in any genuine propositions. Still, despite the preparation we have received for these claims, they are apt to be experienced as too quick. For we might well be inclined to ask: even if Wittgenstein has revealed "object" to be a formal and, therefore, mere pseudo-, concept, how has this been shown of these other central notions? Do we not require further arguments before this much more general conclusion can be properly drawn?

We do, of course, find further discussion of the notion of number in particular in the 6s and to that extent these questions are appropriate. But in a more important sense, I would suggest that they miss the mark entirely. For such questions reflect what we have seen to be a fundamental assumption (whether explicit or implicit) of many Tractarian interpreters – namely, that Wittgenstein is throughout the text attempting to provide *arguments* for controversial and disputable theses. Even for those commentators who nominally reject this reading, who see the *Tractatus* as concerned solely to eliminate philosophical confusions, the tendency is quite strong at these points to attribute to Wittgenstein something like a substantive doctrine. After all, if his ultimate aim really is to show the meaninglessness of all philosophical questions, he must be, as it were, laying his cards on the table when he comes out and *says* this (or something quite near to it). It is quite tempting to suppose that these sorts of utterances must occupy a special position in the framework of the *Tractatus,* to have a unique status.[54]

But temptations only lead us astray in Wittgenstein's austere world and so must be countered. The temptation here is to imagine that "being a formal concept" is put forth as a *criterion* of nonsensicality, a criterion, we then go on to protest, which has not yet been shown to apply to "fact," "number," and so forth. But we must ask ourselves whether this as a criterion has been shown to "apply" even to the notion of an object. That is, is Wittgenstein's method to make clear what an object is and then subsequently to go on to bring out how that concept is, after all, only formal? Our whole discussion thus far has been designed to suggest how this description is not adequate. We have sought to bring out that an understanding of the role of "object" in the *Tractatus is* its recognition as purely formal, that the only philosophical hold we have on this notion is as an intrinsic feature of our way of representing the world. This recognition, in turn, is just the recognition of the nonsensicality (in the *Tractatus'* sense of the term) of the attempt to provide a specification of the object. We might then say that the claim "It is nonsense to seek to represent an object" constitutes, to use the language of the later Wittgenstein, a purely *grammatical* remark. (In Tractarian terms we could say that it is an expression of an internal relation.) The point, in other words, is that our notions of object, formal concept, and philosophical nonsense are all given together, emerging through reflection on the pictorial nature of the proposition and what it would mean to provide an analysis. There can then be no question of offering *criteria* of nonsensicality, of adopting a standpoint from which we can, once and for all, assess the "real character" of our utterances about objects.

By contrast, however, the *Tractatus'* reflection on the nature of the proposition may lead us to understand differently the role of the object; it may bring us to see, as I have suggested above, that the (philosophical) questions we were originally inclined to ask in connection with this notion have lost their allure. Rather than establishing the truth of certain propositions, the task of the *Tractatus* at this juncture could then be described as one of characterizing the philosophical inquiry into objects so thoroughly that it crumbles under its own weight. We do not thereby explain the philosophical perspective or reveal its true nature, but we can come to recognize its precariousness: we *see through* the terms of the *Tractatus.* These terms, moreover, are all of a piece; they are intended to characterize, as I have claimed, a *single* viewpoint.[55] And that means that the insight into the status of one of the central Tractarian notions must be at the same time an insight into the rest. In acknowledging the weakness of our grasp on "object" we are acknowledging the same about "complex," "fact," "function," "number," and so on.

This point becomes even more evident when we notice the phrase "and so on" that follows this list of central notions – the list as Wittgenstein gives it at 4.1272. He plainly is not attempting to provide a complete inventory of formal concepts, to go through all of our misleading notions one by one. Indeed, it would be nonsensical to attempt to do so *a priori,* since the logical forms are said to be "anumerical" (TLP 4.128). Rather, we are meant to see that the same *kind* of move is described in the attempt to inquire into any of these notions, that we are in every case involved in imagining an incoherent detachment from the fabric of our own language. The "and so on," we might say, thus expresses the comprehensiveness of the shift in outlook that the *Tractatus* aims to effect. We do not by means of this text arrive at new, superior accounts of "fact," "object," and "number." What the *Tractatus* seeks instead is to lead us to regard in a new way our attempts to gain clarity about all such notions; it seeks to get us to *go on* differently in our efforts to know the world. We are called to go on without philosophy.

CHAPTER III

THE ESSENCE OF THE PROPOSITION

I

Wittgenstein's attempt to undermine what he sees as the heart of the philosophical endeavor would seem to be already well under way with the completion of his initial account of analysis. It is not, then, that the straightforward attacks on the central notions of logic at 4.1272, 4.1274, and 4.128 – or even his later 6.54 denial of significance to all of his own propositions – represent a sudden shift in the direction of the *Tractatus.* Instead, we have seen that these remarks should be understood as more explicit statements of what is Wittgenstein's fundamental point throughout – or, perhaps better, as indications of how we are to regard the seemingly more metaphysical claims in the earlier sections of the text. If we accept such an interpretation, however, one might well wonder what work is left to be done after the 3s and early 4s. Would not the central steps toward finding "on all essential points, the final solution of the problems" (TLP Preface) of philosophy already have been taken, a third of the way through the *Tractatus?* What, then, is the purpose of the rest of the book? Moreover, one might also wonder how the account that we have given squares with Wittgenstein's subsequent concern to specify the "general form of the proposition" and his claim at 5.471 and 5.4711 that this specification represents the *essence* of the proposition and, indeed, of the world. Would such ideas not imply that the real focus of "logic" is yet to be expounded, that the account up to this juncture is in some sense only preliminary?

We must recall once more the nature of the investigation in which the *Tractatus* is involved. I have suggested that it aims to communicate a single view of the nature of logic, that indeed central to understanding the text (as well as the real character of its subsequent repudiation by Wittgenstein) is appreciating how it is committed to supposing a kind of essence to the perspective it expresses. For Wittgenstein, then, it seems we should say that the *Tractatus'* ultimate point can be grasped in its entirety at *any* juncture of the text. Thus, in a sense, there can be no "preliminary" stages for us to pass through, no overwhelming need to go on once we appear to have grasped its central teaching. The absence of any further work to be done at this stage is then not a criticism but rather just the point.

Nonetheless, the *Tractatus does* continue. This continuation, moreover, is not in any obvious sense a mere repetition of the themes developed in the first part of the text, but instead involves a host of new terms and seemingly new questions, as well as the introduction of various apparent technical moves. If the *Tractatus* is to be seen as setting forth a single unified vision, it is one that evidently requires a good deal of structure to be maintained.[1] Our aim in this chapter is to make as clear as possible the features the 4s, 5s, and 6s add to that increasingly complex structure – the analysis of the logical constants, the truth tables and the idea of logic as tautologous, the specification of the general form of the proposition, and so on. But this "making clear" must involve showing how these details can be regarded as part only of an *extension* of a perspective, rather than the introduction of a fresh set of principles. Our central purpose, in other words, will be to elaborate Wittgenstein's further working out of the "problems of philosophy," while at the same time preserving the sense of the whole endeavor as the expression of a single thought.

II

To set the stage for the discussion that we find in these later sections of the book, we must first return to the initial account of the picture. After reiterating at 2.2 the identity of form between the picture and what it depicts, the next several remarks all deal with a picture's "representing" of a "possibility" of facts:

> The picture depicts reality by representing (*darstellt*) a possibility of the existence and nonexistence of atomic facts. (TLP 2.201)
> The picture represents a possible state of affairs (*Sachlage*) in logical space. (TLP 2.202)

> The picture contains the possibility of the state of affairs it represents. (TLP 2.2.03)

Note first the parallel between these remarks – especially 2.201 – and 2.11: "The picture presents (*vorstellt*) the states of affairs in logical space, the existence and nonexistence of atomic facts." It would seem that a picture "presents" existent and nonexistent atomic facts, but "represents" a *possibility* of such facts. Now I have already suggested[2] that what a picture presents is all those states of affairs it can be used to depict; a picture presents both existent and nonexistent facts because the same picture that allows us to say that some fact A is the case also allows us to say that A is not the case. What a picture represents would then seem to be the choice that is made *among* these facts laid out in logical space; it is, as it were, a possibility drawn from the set.[3]

An example will help to make evident the significance of this distinction between the presenting and representing dimensions of the picture. Let us take the case of a picture depicting a book lying on a table. If we correlate the pictorial book with a real book and the pictorial table with a real table, this picture will be said to "present" both the fact that the book is on the table and the fact that it is not on the table. It "represents," by contrast, some particular state of affairs in logical space, that is to say either the book's lying on the table or it's not doing so (but not both at once). We then ask: what determines which one of these possible states of affairs is in fact represented by the picture in some given case? Wittgenstein develops his answer to this question at some length in the *Notebooks*, as, for example, in these passages from November 1914:

> The picture has whatever relation to reality it does have. And the point is how it is supposed to represent (*darstellen*).[4] The same picture will agree or fail to agree with reality according to how it is supposed to represent. (NB 23) The method of portrayal (*Abbildungsmethode;* method of depicting) must be completely determinate before we can compare reality with the proposition at all in order to see whether it is true or false. The method of comparison must be given me before I can make the comparison. (NB 23)

The point in these passages seems to be that the possibility of a picture's representing some particular state of affairs – and hence its capacity to be true or false – is dependent on the *way* that picture is as a whole compared with reality: it is just our method of comparison that decides whether we understand this picture as holding the book to be on the table or not on the table. And, in the same way, it is the method of comparison that determines whether a more complex picture depicting, say, states of affairs A and B represents A v B, A & ~B, ~A ⊃ B, or any other truth functional combination. With the focus on the representational capacities of the picture, the so-called logical constants thus come to the fore. They are to be construed as the characteristic means of, as Wittgenstein puts it in the *Notebooks,* "project[ing] the picture of the elementary proposition on to reality" (NB 29).

It is important to see how, according to this story, the possibility of applying any one of the logical constants might be said to presuppose the ability to apply all the rest. For the picture represents always a selection *within* the field of what it presents, as one might put it. Wittgenstein then attempts to bring out the sense in which that "field" is present in its entirety as soon as we have a picture of the world. This is what he has in mind, for example, at 3.42: "Although a proposition may only determine one place in logical space, the whole logical space must already be given by it. (Otherwise denial, the logical sum, the logical product, etc., would always introduce new elements – in co-ordination)." Part of the reason for this claim we have already alluded to in our brief discussion of negation.[5] For in pointing out that a picture of some fact A can be used to assert ~A, we are really saying that both facts are given together: if we know what it means for the book to be on the table we at the same time know what it is for it *not* to be on the table. That negative fact, moreover, is not some brute gesture toward the totality of things not identical with books on tables, as if we were supposing that the negation of A includes, besides ~A, also B, C, D and so forth. Instead, the denied picture carves out a *distinct* state of affairs, occupying its own position in logical space. This whole idea is perhaps stated most clearly and succinctly at 4.0641:

> One could say, the denial is already related to the logical place determined by the proposition that is denied. The denying proposition determines a logical place *other* than does the proposition denied. The denying proposition determines a logical place, with the help of the proposition denied, by saying that it lies outside the latter place. That one can deny again the denied proposition, shows that what is denied is already a proposition and not merely the preliminary to a proposition.

Now although there is one sign for negation in the language, say, of *Principia Mathematica,* we should not be misled by this into supposing that "~p" specifies a unique way of comparing the proposition with reality. For, as Wittgenstein later points out, "~~~p" will represent this same fact, as will "~p v ~p," "p⊃ ~p," and so on: "That which denies in "*~p*" is however not "~," but that which all signs of this notation, which deny *p,* have in common. Hence the common rule according to which "*~p,*" "*~~~p,*" "*~p* v *~p,*" "*~p* & *~p,*" etc. etc. (to infinity) are constructed" (TLP 5.512).

But this then suggests that to understand denial we must also understand all the other logical constants,[6] and in every context in which they could occur. Thus Wittgenstein remarks on how the proposition "reaches through the *whole* of logical space" (TLP 3.42; emphasis mine). Thus, too, he regards the possibility of the Sheffer stroke (which by itself constitutes a truth-functionally complete set) as of great significance, and makes use of it in his characterization of the general form of the proposition: it serves as a way of expressing just the essential interconnectiveness of all our means of representing the world.

Wittgenstein's basic thought here would thus seem to be that, given any picture, any means of depiction, everything we can say about the world is in some sense laid out in advance – we know at once *all* the possibilities of the existence and nonexistence of atomic facts that it could represent. The logical constants, as the means of specifying various subsets within that set of possibilities presented by the picture, then enable us to assert some *particular* state of affairs as the case. They allow us, that is, to make a claim that can be judged true or false and hence will be involved in any proposition we make about the world.

It is, I suggest, just because the capacity to say something true or false could be seen in this way to depend on a prior set of unasserted possibilities that Wittgenstein in the *Notebooks* connects his conception with (what he understands as) Frege's idea of the "assumption":

> Although all logical constants must already occur in the simple proposition, its own peculiar proto-picture (*Urbild*) *must* surely also occur in it whole and undivided. Then is the picture perhaps not the simple proposition, but rather its prototype (*Urbild*) which must occur in it? Then, this prototype is not actually a proposition (though it has the Gestalt of a proposition) and it might correspond to Frege's "assumption"

> (*Annahme*). In that case the proposition would consist of proto-*pictures,* which were projected on to the world. (NB 29–30)

Wittgenstein is here presumably referring to Frege's claim that a judgment involves a movement from a "mere combination of ideas" (BEG 11) – an unaffirmed thought marked in the *Begriffsschrift* by a horizontal stroke – to a statement that is asserted as true (which in the *Begriffsschrift* will then be prefaced by "|–," the so-called judgment stroke). Commentators have long been puzzled about Wittgenstein's interest in (and interpretation of) this Fregean idea, which he refers to not only in the *Notebooks* but also at 4.063 of the *Tractatus.*[7] But with the above discussion, the connection to Wittgenstein's own concerns should now start to become clear. What the *Notebooks* passage calls the "proto-picture" would seem to be equivalent to the existent and non-existent atomic facts that the picture presents, or, rather, what is common to those facts. Since it is only with the determinate method of projection provided by the logical constants that the picture can represent a particular state of affairs – that is, assert something as the case – we might well regard the proto-picture as akin to the Fregean "assumption."[8]

Of course, this is by no means to suggest that Wittgenstein's thinking here should simply be assimilated to Frege's. Rather, Wittgenstein, in his characteristic way of responding to his predecessors, must be understood essentially as *coopting* the Fregean insight, taking what he sees as important in Frege's approach and using it toward a very un-Fregean end. What is important in the notion of the assumption for Wittgenstein is that it brings out how the possibility of saying something determinate about the world depends logically on a prior inner connection between language and reality, a form that is common to both. At the same time, a clear understanding of this idea makes evident that we have no hold on that form apart from our capacity to make true and false statements about the world.

Just this idea would seem ultimately to lie behind remarks 4.063 and 4.064, which I think it is useful to quote in full:

> An illustration (*Bild;* "picture") to explain the concept of truth. A black spot on white paper; the form of the spot can be described by saying of each point of the plane whether it is white or black. To the fact that a point is black corresponds a positive fact; to the fact that a point is white (not black), a negative fact. If I indicate a point of the plane (a truth-

> value in Frege's terminology), this corresponds to the assumption (*Annahme*) proposed for judgment, etc. etc.
>
> But to be able to say that a point is black or white, I must first know under what conditions a point is called white or black; in order to be able to say "p" is true (or false) I must have determined under what conditions I call "p" true, and thereby I determine the sense of the proposition.
>
> The point at which the simile breaks down is this: we can indicate a point on the paper, without knowing what white and black are; but to a proposition without a sense corresponds nothing at all, for it signifies no thing (truth-value) whose properties are called "false" or "true"; the verb of the proposition is not "is true" or "is false" – as Frege thought – but that which "is true" must already contain the verb. (TLP 4.063)
>
> Every proposition must *already* have a sense; assertion cannot give it a sense, for what it asserts is the sense itself. And the same holds of denial, etc. (TLP 4.064)

Now Wittgenstein's conception of truth will be discussed in more detail shortly. But it would be easy to conclude from these passages that he is primarily concerned to advance an extreme form of verificationism, that his contention is that for a proposition to have a sense we must first lay down some sort of rule specifying the conditions under which it is to count as true. Such an idea, however, runs fundamentally counter to what we have described as Wittgenstein's conception of the self-sufficiency of sense, the notion that, as he puts it at 5.473, "logic must take care of itself."[9] Instead, we must view this passage in connection with his earlier discussion of the picture.

The claim at 2.17, we recall, is that the *Form der Abbildung,* the pictorial form, is identical in the picture and what it depicts: because the pictorial elements have the same possibilities of combination as the objects for which they go proxy the picture will always be a picture of the world. It is then against the background of this common pictorial space that the picture can be projected so as to specify a determinate state of affairs. In the terms of the above passage, this idea could be expressed by saying that it is only given the possibility of identifying a location on the piece of paper (the analogue to the Fregean *Annahme*) that I can assert that a given point is black or not black. Then, just as the possibility of representing a state of affairs requires a particular way of projecting the picture, Wittgenstein here points out that the possibility of making a determinate assertion in the case at hand demands our knowing what it means for a point to be black or white. This, however, is not analogous to some special stipulation that must accompany the proposition but, rather, describes what it means to have a proposition in the first place: the proposition *is* the setting forth of a possibility of a state of affairs, the identifying (with the help of the logical constants) of a particular region in logical space.[10] That is why Wittgenstein emphasizes that, unlike in the analogy of the spot on the paper, there is nothing that corresponds to the assumption in the case of the proposition without a sense – we do not first point to a region in logical space and then decide whether it or its negation is to be asserted. Instead, to have a proposition is just to have provided ourselves with the *means* of arriving at what could be the case, of specifying a sense. What Wittgenstein sees Frege as (appropriately) reaching for with his talk of the "entertaining" of a thought is then the idea that the logical constants cannot accomplish this end on their own, that they must be conceived as in some sense operations on a pregiven content. Frege's confusion, however, is to suppose that this "pregiven content" is itself a kind of determination of reality, rather than only the condition of such a possibility. Thus, Wittgenstein says that the genuine proposition already has a sense – no further move is required for it to represent a determinate state of affairs.

Through this discussion we then begin to see the thinness of the notion of a "logical constant." For to hold that the proposition already has a sense, or that the whole of logical space is given along with the picture (and what it presents) is to suggest that the logical constants do not introduce anything *new* into our understanding of the world. Once we have the picture with its intrinsic connection to the world, it would seem that everything that is of significance for logic is already given: logic comprehends only *how* reality becomes determined. Hence Wittgenstein's oft-quoted remark: "My fundamental thought is that the "logical constants" do not represent (*vertreten*). That the *logic* of the facts cannot be represented" (TLP 4.0312). Now Ogden's rendering of *vertreten* here as "represent" is somewhat misleading, particularly given my own translation of *darstellen* by this word. I suggest that "deputize for" or "stand for" would be a better, if more awkward, translation, since (as we have seen) the term *vertreten* is also used at 2.131 to characterize the relation between the pictorial elements and the objects with which they are correlated. It then becomes apparent that Wittgenstein's point is that the logical constants cannot be construed as *names,* as additional elements of the proposition to which there must correspond anything in the world. We correlate elements of the proposition with objects and, given the pictorial nature of the proposition, are then at once able to represent the full range of possible facts – no *logical* coordination is necessary.

For Wittgenstein, then, the true import of Frege's distinction between assumption and assertion is just the dismantling of the most fundamental Fregean idea – the idea that "logic" constitutes a genuine subject matter. We are meant to see that, contrary to Frege's contention, the logical functions cannot be construed along the lines of genuine (material) functions, that it makes no sense to suppose a domain of entities which form the special province of the logician. Nor is this a point directed merely at Frege. Russell is even more explicitly committed to the assumption of a definite logical subject matter, as is evident in his previously referred to claim that "the chief part of philosophical logic" is "the endeavor to see clearly the entities" that mathematics regards as indefinable (*Principles* xv). He in fact goes so far as to compare the attempt to grasp the fundamental concepts of logic with the search for Neptune, "with the difference that the final stage – the search with a mental telescope for the entity which has been inferred – is often the most difficult part of the undertaking" (*Principles* xv). Russell's approach, too, is called into question with the *Tractatus'* attempt to deflate the reality of the logical constants.

Still, one may wonder why this claim of Wittgenstein's should constitute his "fundamental thought." Surely there is more at issue in the *Tractatus* than whether or not "and," "or," "not," and so on stand for anything. Indeed, there is surely much more going on in *Frege* and *Russell* than the bare assertion of the existence of such entities. Perhaps the undermining of this assumption does call into question the "Platonism" inherent in the Fregean and Russellian approaches – but that alone would hardly serve to cast aspersion on the sum total of their contributions. Why, then, is the "nonrepresentativeness" of the logical constants held to be such a central point?

Part of the answer, at least, has to do with the *sort* of move that Wittgenstein is here making. For in holding that nothing corresponds to the logical constants, he really must be understood as attempting to show, in a manner analogous to his treatment of the elementary propositions, the misguidedness of the philosopher's demand more generally. Just as the *Bedeutungen* of the names were seen to be absorbed into the way the propositional constituent functions in the propositions in which it can appear, so the logical constants are incorporated into the means by which the propositional sign as a whole is compared with reality. Wittgenstein is then suggesting that the attempt to "look for" a logical entity of the Fregean/Russellian variety is not a mere *vain* endeavor – as if he were claiming, to use Russell's analogy, that the location in space in which we hoped to find a planet is in fact empty – but a *chimera:* it is nonsense to suppose that an "it" could ever satisfy our search. And that makes it evident that the ultimate point here is much the same as the one that emerged in the discussion of the analysis of the elementary proposition. The move against the logical constants can thus be said to be paradigmatic of the *Tractatus'* way of dissolving the questions of philosophy (in particular, the sorts of questions that Wittgenstein takes Frege and Russell to be concerned with) and in this sense to be its "fundamental" thought.

Indeed, the *Tractatus' Grundgedanke* is explicitly anticipated in the remarks that close the 3s:

> The proposition determines a place in logical space: the existence of this logical place is guaranteed by the existence of the constituent parts alone, by the existence of the significant proposition. (TLP 3.4)
> The propositional sign and the logical coordinates: that is the logical place. (TLP 3.41)
> The geometrical and the logical place agree in that each is a possibility of an existence. (TLP 3.411)

The "logical place," it would appear, is nothing but some state of affairs (a *possible* fact) that the proposition can represent; it is one position within the overall coordinate system that Wittgenstein calls logical space. In asserting that such a place is "guaranteed" by the existence of the significant proposition, Wittgenstein must then be seen as again emphasizing the internal nature of the relation between a proposition and what it represents: the proposition is nothing but the stipulating of a location within a larger framework and hence cannot but pick out a logical place. The logical constants or "logical coordinates," as the particular ways that the propositional sign is projected on to the world, constitute part of the means by which that stipulation becomes possible. But that is to say that the logical constants, instead of constituting some features of reality that might themselves be described, simply form part of the logical coordinate system within which genuine descriptions are made.

The idea of the coordinate system is thus again central in Wittgenstein's attempt to show the emptiness of the philosophical enterprise. Still, while this image brings out rather strikingly how the logical constants cannot be blithely included in amongst the other elements of the world, it may appear to do so at the price of assuming a very inflated conception of "logical space." For does not the notion that the whole of logical space is somehow "given in its entirety" with the possibility of a proposition express nearly everything that philosophers have traditionally meant when they have held logic to be *a priori?* Has Wittgenstein then not simply transposed the question of the nature of the supposed logical entities to onc about the nature of this mysterious *a priori* coordinate system – logical space?

In fact, Wittgenstein's full answer to this question is bound up with his understanding of the logical constants as operations and hence must await our discussion of the specification of the general form of the proposition. But the general direction of his response should already become apparent when we recall what it really means for him to say that the picture presents the existence and nonexistence of atomic facts. For this is simply a way of pointing out that it is the same picture that allows us to say A and also ~A, A & B as well as ~A v B, and so on: the whole account of the picture, we must remember, assumes from the start the notion of the picture *in use*. The "field" of what a picture presents – logical space itself – then grows out of, is parasitic on, what that picture can represent, by means of the logical constants. Thus Wittgenstein, one sentence after declaring that the "whole logical space must already be given" by the proposition, adds: "The logical scaffolding round the picture *determines* the logical space" (TLP 3.42; emphasis mine). The case, in other words, is in many respects the same as with physical space: just as we saw that the form of physical space does not constitute an *a priori* constraint on our ability to represent the world but, rather, emerges out of the significant use of the spatial picture, so too with logical space and the logical picture. Logical space, we might say, is the necessary *by-product* of our ability to represent the world.

This is not to deny that, in a certain sense, the contours of logical space can be described in advance. The existence of logical inference, as the *Tractatus* understands it, depends on such a possibility. Indeed, the same possibility allows Wittgenstein himself to offer his own general characterization of the proposition.[11] But, as we shall see, the central purpose of that characterization is to make clear how we nonetheless cannot understand the dimensions of logical space entirely apart from the use, the projection of the proposition. Wittgenstein's aim is thus not to deny altogether the traditional idea of logic as *a priori*, but to attain greater clarity with regard to that notion. And that, for him, will mean precisely showing how *little* the *a priori* comes to: it comprehends no more than our characteristic methods of projecting the pictorial fact on to reality.

III

Here, though, Tractarian readers of a certain mindset may well balk. For I seem to be suggesting that talk of "projection" constitutes, as it were, the end of the story for Wittgenstein – as if seeing how the logical dimensions of the proposition are incorporated into the projecting of our pictures were akin to those dimensions' vanishing from the radar screen of philosophical consideration. But doesn't the *Tractatus* in fact hold that the possibility of projection itself requires explanation? And is the notion of "thinking" not introduced to fulfill just this function?[12] After all, Wittgenstein follows the above quoted series of claims with a remark about the "applied, thought (*gedachte;* "thought-through"), propositional sign" (TLP 3.5) and, at 3.11, explicitly equates thinking with a kind of projection. It might well seem that Wittgenstein, in a manner reminiscent of Frege, is fundamentally committed to the assumption of a kind of mental intermediary between language and the world – that it is indeed against precisely this picture that much of the anti-mentalism of the *Investigations* is directed.[13]

To attribute this conception to the *Tractatus* would give its move against the assumption of genuine logical constants a quite different character than what I have been suggesting. We must then examine more closely Wittgenstein's way of connecting the notions of proposition, thought, and projection.

> In the proposition (*Satz*) the thought is expressed perceptibly through the senses. (TLP 3.1)

> We use the sensibly perceptible sign (sound or written sign, etc.) of the proposition as a projection of the possible state of affairs. The method of projection is the thinking of the sense of the proposition. (TLP 3.11)
> The sign through which we express the thought I call the propositional sign. And the proposition is the propositional sign in its projective relation to the world. (TLP 3.12)
> The thought is the significant proposition. (*der sinnvolle Satz;* TLP 4)

The thought – the logical picture of the world – is in these passages presented as intimately connected to the proposition; it is, we might say, just by means of the proposition that the thought is expressed, made manifest. The proposition, in turn, cannot be understood apart from the propositional sign in its significant use. Thus, rather than having two entities – the thought and the propositional sign – and then worrying over how they are to be connected, for Wittgenstein the thought would seem to emerge precisely in and through the projection of the propositional sign on to reality.

The contrast of this approach with Frege's is at once apparent. For Frege (post-1892), the proposition (*Satz*), like the name, has both a sense (*Sinn*) and a reference (*Bedeutung*). The proposition's *Bedeutung* is a truth value, its *Sinn,* a thought. While the relation between a propositional sign and a thought is on this account somewhat obscure – the latter presumably cannot be *named* by the propositional sign, since then it would constitute its *Bedeutung* – Frege over and over insists on the independent, genuine existence of the *Gedanke.*[14] For him, this assumption is unavoidable if the objectivity of language – which is to say the possibility of science, of communication in general – is to be secured.

Far from adopting a Fregean model of the relation of thought and propositional sign, it begins to seem as if the *Tractatus* is essentially concerned to advance a diametrically opposed conception. In introducing the notion of the projected propositional sign, Wittgenstein would appear to be suggesting that it is simply unnecessary to assume the existence of a separate thought, a vaporous "proposition," hovering over the propositional sign. His ultimate aim, we might then suppose, is just to restrict Frege's extravagant ontology, to propose a counter theory in which the thought is "immanent" in the propositional sign.

But to put the matter this way is now to overstate Wittgenstein's difference with Frege – or, rather, to misdescribe the real character of that difference. For one thing, it appears to leave Wittgenstein open to the charge of subjectivism (one thinks here of Frege's objections against formalism): to simply *deny* the existence of the Fregean *Gedanke* would seemingly be to reject the objectivity it is supposed to guarantee. The embrace of subjectivism, however, is not only very foreign to the *Tractatus* in general but also specifically ignores the extent to which Wittgenstein seeks to accommodate a notion of objectivity within his conceptions of thought and thinking:

> We cannot think anything unlogical, for otherwise we should have to think unlogically. (TLP 3.03)
>
> It used to be said that God could create everything, except what was contrary to the laws of logic. The truth is, we could not *say* of an "unlogical" world how it would look. (TLP 3.031)
>
> That logic is *a priori* consists in the fact that we *cannot* think illogically. (TLP 5.4731)

Indeed, these passages have a distinctly Fregean ring to them, in particular hearkening back to the *Grundgesetze* discussion of our supposed inability to understand beings "whose laws of thought flatly contradicted ours" (BLA 14).[15] Wittgenstein's relation to Frege on the issue of the nature of thinking evidently cannot be construed in terms of flatly opposed positions.

One solution to these interpretational difficulties would be to see the *Tractatus* as retaining the Fregean notion of thought, but, in effect, purging it of any connection with ontology. That is, Wittgenstein is to be understood as seeking to account for what one might think of as the objective dimension of language – in effect, the possibility of successful communication – but to express that only in logical, rather than ontological terms. In this sense he could be said to be getting at the heart of Frege's view, since one might well argue that, for the latter, the real criterion of identity for thoughts ultimately is given by a sentence's role in logical inference patterns.

Now such an interpretation is, I would suggest, correct as far as it goes. But even here we must caution against a too facile incorporation of Wittgenstein's views within a Fregean framework. For while the *Tractatus* retains Fregean language regarding the normative status of logical laws, its central aim is always to shift our understanding of what that normativity comes to. The nature of this shift is already apparent in the remark following 3.031, the remark about the impossibility of illogical thought quoted above: "To represent (*darstellen*) in language anything which 'contradicts logic' is as impossible as in geometry to represent by its co-ordinates a figure which contradicts the laws of space; or to give the co-ordinates of a point which does not exist" (TLP 3.032). Why can't we give the coordinates of a point which does not exist? The answer, of course, is that to specify coordinates on a graph *is* to specify a point. This is not to attribute some magical creative properties to such a specification, but is simply a way of bringing out that we do not have a notion of a point apart from the way it is, or rather could be, identified. The same will then be said to hold with regard to "thinking" and "region within logical space." We might assert that to think is always to specify a region in logical space, but that is just because the projecting of the pictorial fact on to reality – its being thought – *structures* this space, the logical coordinate system: thinking and logic, we could say, are given together.

Wittgenstein thus attempts to preserve the Fregean insight about the impossibility of illogical thought – even, as I suggested above, to get at the heart of what he takes to be Frege's concern. Once more, though, it becomes apparent how, for the *Tractatus*, the exposing of the heart of a philosophical question is equivalent to its disappearance; the *necessity* that is said to belong to thought's respecting of logical boundaries comes at the price of the utter emptiness of this claim. We might then express Wittgenstein's general stance toward the notions of thought and thinking in this way. Clearly, he is not concerned to dispute the assertion that there is thinking, that the propositional sign is not capable of interpreting itself. Of course we think. The real question concerns the significance of this truism, the suitability of the notions of thinking and thought for use as central tools of philosophical analysis. What Wittgenstein aims to bring out is how the significant proposition with which we begin any analysis is *already* "thought," how we *start out* with "the propositional sign in its projective relation to the world." This idea, as we have seen, informs every aspect of his discussion of the picture: the picture's capacity to represent some particular state of affairs presupposes the projecting both of the pictorial elements (the possibilities of which constitute the picture's *Form der Abbildung*), and the pictorial fact (the possibilities of which constitute logical space) on to reality. Thinking permeates the picture – and so the possibilities for one of these notions cannot but coincide with the possibilities for the other. But that at the same time expresses the *weakness* of our hold on the notion of thinking; it brings out how "thought" is no closer to us, so to speak, than the logic it would clarify. Far from postulating a mental bridge connecting the picture to reality, as Hacker suggests,[16] Wittgenstein suggests that it is the mental realm itself that needs to be accessed – and the way is via the picture.

IV

Still, if "thinking" will not play an explanatorily privileged role in the *Tractatus'* discussion of logical space, we must come to understand how, for Wittgenstein, we *can* characterize this latter notion and what such a characterization comes to. We shall address this issue through a consideration first of the *Tractatus'* notion of tautology and then of its specification of the general form of the proposition.

Both of these notions may be approached through further reflection on the Tractarian conception of "sense" and its relation to "truth." These central terms are introduced at the close of Wittgenstein's initial discussion of the picture. First, then, 2.221: "What the picture represents is its sense (*Sinn*)." Since, as we have seen, the picture is also said to "represent" some particular state of affairs in logical space, this suggests that such an assemblage of facts is to be regarded as the sense of that picture. 4.031 confirms the point: "One can say, instead of, This proposition has such and such a sense, This proposition represents (*darstellt*) such and such state of affairs (*Sachlage*)." Which state of affairs is then to be identified with the picture/proposition's sense? It may appear as if Wittgenstein gives conflicting responses to this question. For at 4.063, he suggests that the sense is given through knowing what obtains when the proposition is true: "In order to be able to say 'p' is true (or false) I must have determined under what conditions I call 'p' true, and thereby I determine the sense of the proposition."[17] It appears from 4.2, however, that I only know a proposition's sense when I know what it means to be true *and* false: "The sense of a proposition is its agreement and disagreement with the possibilities of the existence and nonexistence of the atomic facts"; sense here includes all of a proposition's truth-possibilities. This appearance of conflict disappears, however, when we recall from our earlier discussion[18] that the *Sachlage* represented by the proposition is itself conceived as containing both an existent and nonexistent atomic fact – that is, a positive and negative fact. The *Sachlage*, in other words, is what Wittgenstein at 4.063 likens to a solid substance and the space within it, in which a body may be placed. To represent a sense is then to highlight, as it were, one of the twin aspects presented by the picture.[19] But that highlighting always takes place against the backdrop of its complement – which is to say that an understanding of the proposition's truth conditions carries with it an understanding of its falsification conditions and vice versa. As Wittgenstein remarks at 3.144, the sense of a proposition is like an arrow, orienting us in *this* way toward the facts with which it is associated.

Now taken in isolation, these claims may seem to commit Wittgenstein to a kind of realism of facts reminiscent of Russell's logical atomism.[20] After all, one might ask, is he not suggesting that a prior cognizance of a fact (or set of facts) is necessary to understand the picture's sense – and, therefore, that facts, possible as well as actual, must be assumed to be brutely "out there"? And are not these facts regarded as responsible for "making" the picture (or proposition) true or false?[21] Given what we have said about the first part of the picture theory alone, however, it should be clear that Wittgenstein cannot intend to maintain any such position. The pictorial elements and their real world counterparts are held to have the same possibilities of combination: the force of this assertion, we have seen, is to bring out the inseparability of the connection between the picture and reality, to suggest that the fact is only given, only structured or shaped, through the picture that depicts it. Wittgenstein, rather than endorsing a full-blown Russellian ontology of facts – positive, negative, particular, general, and so forth – is thus from the start seeking to bring out the emptiness of this whole conception. (We must not forget, after all, that 4.1272 declares any talk of facts to be *nonsense*.) In identifying a picture/proposition's sense with a state of affairs, he should then be seen really as stressing the flip side of what 4.014 refers to as the "pictorial internal relation which holds between language and the world." That is, just as earlier he emphasizes how we can have no hold on "fact" apart from the particular means we use to represent the world, at this point he is stressing how our understanding of the nature of that means of representation is likewise inseparable from the facts toward which it is directed.

This, of course, is not to suggest that there is no way in which the world and the picture can be compared. On the contrary, it is just because some kind of comparison can be effected that we are able to speak of truth or falsity at all. Nonetheless, we must recognize how we come to this point only *after* every move having to do with the logic of depiction has been taken. 2.173 helps to clarify this point: "A picture represents its subject from a position outside it. (Its standpoint is its representational form [*Form der Darstellung*]). That is why a picture represents its subject correctly or incorrectly." The *Form der Darstellung* comprises the various ways of projecting the picture on to reality (the various ways, that is to say, that a picture can *represent*); the picture can be said to stand "outside" its subject matter because the method of projection always operates on a completed picture, as it were, on the pictorial elements taken against the background of the *Form der Abbildung*.[22] Given that this form is common to the picture and what it depicts, the whole space of facts presented by the picture will necessarily belong to the world. Once the picture is then projected in a determinate manner, it will represent exactly one state of affairs as obtaining, fixing what we are to expect to the extent that, as Wittgenstein later puts it, "one only needs to say 'Yes' or 'No' to [the picture] to make it agree with reality" (TLP 4.023). The "yes" or "no," of course, corresponds to the picture's truth or falsity. But since what the world will look like in either case has been completely described beforehand, this verdict is, so to speak, an easy call – it is simply a matter of looking.

To refer to the *Tractatus'* remarks about truth as constituting a "correspondence theory," as is typically done,[23] is then not wrong, but it potentially misses the point. For this phrase might tend to suggest some sort of agreement between two distinct sets of facts, while Wittgenstein's primary aim, as I have indicated, is to show just the intrinsic connection between the picture's content and the world: it is precisely because a possible state of affairs is, as he puts at 2.203, "contained" in the picture that any sort of agreement between the two can be realized. The claim about the need to compare the picture and reality, rather than constituting part of an elaborate correspondence theory, is thus really meant to drive a wedge between the notion of truth and any concern with sense and the conditions of representation (the proper concerns of the philosopher). Wittgenstein's purpose, in other words, is to get us to see that the role of the picture is only to prepare us to meet reality, to enable us to say how things *might* stand – that how things are in fact is not something that can be gathered from the picture alone. It may be helpful to reflect here on Wittgenstein's alternate metaphor of the ruler. To postulate an *a priori* true picture would be like postulating a measurement that is correct simply in virtue of its constituting a position on the measuring scale. But that is nonsense: we have genuinely taken a measurement – we can speak of "correct" and "incorrect" measurements – only when the ruler has been laid *against* some object in the world, if only from afar. In the same way, the picture requires its corresponding reality, the possibility of its being compared to something outside itself, if it is to have the chance of being judged as true.

Wittgenstein makes this idea explicit at the close of his initial discussion of the picture: "It cannot be discovered from the picture alone whether it is true or false. There is no picture which is *a priori* true" (TLP 2.224–5). A picture that does not require comparison with reality will *eo ipso* not represent a possible state of affairs in the world – that is, will not have a sense – and hence will not be a genuine picture. Now for the *Tractatus* the primary, indeed sole, examples of such *a priori* true pseudo-pictures are, of course, the "statements" of formal logic. Implicit in the picture theory, then, is Wittgenstein's later disparagement of the sentences of logic – the "tautologies" and "contradictions" – as "senseless" (*sinnlos;* see TLP 4.461, 4.4611, 5.132).

4.462 makes quite evident how this central idea of the *Tractatus* is connected with the earlier remarks about the picture:

> Tautology and contradiction are not pictures of the reality. They represent (*darstellen*) no possible state of affairs. For the one allows *every* possible state of affairs, the other *none.* In the tautology the conditions of agreement with the world – the representing relations (*die darstellenden Beziehung*) – cancel one another, so that it stands in no representing relation to reality.

The "representing relations," as the various ways in which the picture can be compared with reality, are equivalent to what we have earlier referred to as the methods of projection of the pictorial fact. Wittgenstein is suggesting that, while some method of projection is necessary if a proposition is to represent a particular state of affairs in logical space, in certain instances these methods come in conflict. Suppose, for example, we construct a string of signs of the form p v~p: it is as if, to build on Wittgenstein's metaphor at 4.463, the space that is carved out by p is immediately filled in with the "solid substance" that bounds it; the resulting proposition thus leaves reality absolutely untouched. (Although we might be pleased with such a result from an environmental perspective, from the standpoint of communication it is less than optimal.) Hence "p v ~p" will not say anything, is a tautology and not a genuine proposition, even while it relies on the same rules that enable, for example, "p v ~q" to represent. The very thing that allows propositions to express a definite sense can also serve, it would seem, to deprive them of that sense. For this reason Wittgenstein denies that logical propositions can be completely excluded from a language: "Tautology and contradiction are, however, not nonsensical (*unsinning*); they are part of the symbolism, in the same way that "0" is part of the symbolism of Arithmetic" (TLP 4.4611). For this reason too (or, at least, in part for this reason) he speaks of language as "disguis[ing] thought" (TLP 4.002) and praises Russell for "hav[ing] shown that the apparent logical form of the proposition need not be its real form" (TLP 4.0031): just because "p v ~p" and "p v ~q" have superficially the same form (rely on the same method of projection), we should not at once assume that these are propositions of the same sort. Sense and senselessness spring from the same root and so care must be taken – thoughtfulness exercised – to tease them apart.

This idea of what we might call the delicacy of sense is quite central and needs to be elaborated on. First, it should be noted that the basic point applies not only to the propositions of logic but also to the nonsensical claims of philosophy, albeit in a somewhat different way. To be sure, *Unsinnigkeit* is said in the *Tractatus* to arise not from conflict between the picture's "representing relations," but from a failure to construct a picture in the first place; in such cases, Wittgenstein says, "we have given no *meaning* (*Bedeutung*) to some of [the proposition's] constituent parts" (TLP 5.4733).[24] Nonetheless, like the propositions of logic, most of these pseudo-propositions – and certainly all those that Wittgenstein is chiefly concerned to expose (e.g., "1 is a number," or "There are objects") – have the appearance of ordinary sentences. Indeed, as I pointed out in the Introduction,[25] they would not otherwise have the capacity to mislead. The discernment of what Wittgenstein calls "nonsense" then requires a sensitivity to the multiplicity of logical forms, the good judgment to be able to recognize when the inner syntax of the proposition has been violated. We could say that the central purpose of the discussion of analysis in the 3s is in fact to make precisely this point: to hold that the forms of the elementary propositions are not give *a priori* is just to suggest that sense is not given simply by virtue of a sentence's assuming a particular appearance.[26] The *Tractatus* does not and could not attempt to provide us with an external *mark* of significance.

Of course, all of this is simply a different way of putting what has been my fundamental contention throughout – namely, that the *Tractatus'* method is essentially dialectical, that its aim is always to undermine the central questions of philosophy from the inside, without making appeal to any kind of fixed criteria of sense and nonsense. Still, the difficulties and peculiarities of this whole approach are particularly evident when we focus on the analysis of the propositions of logic. For it would seem that the assertion of the tautological nature of such propositions – the fact that they say nothing about the world – is central to the Tractarian response to the *Principia* and *Begriffsschrift;* Wittgenstein appears to rely on this point as having been firmly established. But we must ask ourselves: How has this been accomplished? It is one thing to grant that a form of words cannot be recognized as a proposition of logic simply from its superficial appearance, but quite another to suppose that, once such a proposition has somehow been identified, one *must* regard it as *sinnlos,* as representing no state of affairs. Has Wittgenstein actually shown that the propositions of logic have this property? At 4.466, he asserts: "In other words, propositions that are true for every state of affairs cannot be combinations of signs at all, since, if they were, only determinate (*bestimmte;* perhaps "particular" would be better here) combinations of objects could correspond to them." But *why* does the fact that "p v ~p" pictures no particular or determinate state of affairs necessarily prevent this expression from composing a legitimate combination of signs?[27] Could we not equally say that such symbols just constitute very *general* pictures? One might suppose that Wittgenstein would buttress his argument with the claim in 6.113: "It is the characteristic mark of logical propositions that one can perceive in the symbol alone that they are true; and this fact contains in itself the whole philosophy of logic." But if this claim rests on the possibility of a general decision procedure for the whole of logic – if, that is, all logical propositions fail to be pictures of the world for the reason that we are imagined to have an *a priori* test for their truth and falsity[28] – then this part of Wittgenstein's argument seems to fall to the ground. For we cannot have a general decision procedure even for all of first order logic, as was shown by Church and Turing in 1936.

The question, then, would appear to stand: How has Wittgenstein *proven* that logical propositions are senseless tautologies?

The answer, of course, is that he has not proven this, any more than he has proven that the world (really) is all that is the case; as I have maintained throughout, "proof" has no place in the philosophical space in which the *Tractatus* moves. But to grasp fully what this general point comes to in this case, we need to consider the more extended discussion of tautology in the 6.1s. Toward the beginning of that discussion Wittgenstein states:

> Theories which make a proposition of logic appear substantial are always false. One could e.g. believe that the words "true" and "false" signify two properties among other properties, and then it would appear as a remarkable fact that every proposition possesses one of these properties. This now by no means appears self-evident, no more so than the proposition "All roses are either yellow or red" would sound even if it were true. Indeed our proposition now gets quite the character of a proposition of natural science and this is a certain symptom of its being falsely understood. (TLP 6.111)

Here Wittgenstein is, in essence, laying down conditions of material adequacy for an analysis of the logical proposition: any acceptable analysis must make evident how such propositions are not true and false like the "substantial" propositions of natural science. Indeed, that analysis also must reveal how the strings of logic are not genuine propositions in the first place since, as he implies in this passage (and has earlier made clear in the discussion of the picture), the possibility of truth and falsity and propositionhood are given together, are internally related. What is important about this passage, then, is that it makes evident that Wittgenstein makes no pretense of being driven by certain previously unrecognized facts, by some overpowering argument, to declare the special nature of the logical proposition. Rather, he *starts off* with the belief that this sort of proposition cannot be approached as if it were on par with a claim of natural science and then attempts to find various means to make this distinction compelling, to persuade us to look at "p v ~p" from other than this "false" ("misleading" would perhaps be a better word here) perspective. The recognition of something peculiar about the status of logical propositions is, in other words, integral to the whole perspective the *Tractatus* seeks to articulate. But that would already seem to indicate that the Tractarian claim about those propositions' tautological nature cannot be viewed simply as a self-standing assertion that awaits its proper justification.

It is in this context, then, that Wittgenstein makes the above-quoted remark (TLP 6.113) about the "truth" of the logical proposition being perceivable in the symbol alone. Now because of this claim, as well as claims like 6.126 ("Whether a proposition belongs to logic can be calculated by calculating the logical properties of the *symbol*."), a number of commentators have assumed that the *Tractatus'* whole position rests on the assumption of a general decision procedure, a point we alluded to above. Of course, Wittgenstein explicitly acknowledges that his "intuitive method" of exposing tautologies – a method that is essentially equivalent to the use of truth tables – is applicable "in cases in which no sign of generality occurs in the tautology" (TLP 6.1203); he certainly does not *seem* to imagine himself as having provided a technique that is applicable to the whole of logic.[29] Regardless, though, even if he did assume that a general decision procedure were available, we must ask ourselves what consequences this mistake would have. Must we conclude, like Black, that it would prove "fatal to Wittgenstein's philosophy of logic"?[30]

A consideration of this question will help to make clearer the *Tractatus'* stance on this whole matter. Let us suppose, counterfactually, that we do have an effective method of determining validity for all of first order logic. We then would stand in the same relation to the whole of logic as we do at present to the propositional calculus. With regard to the latter we now can ask: does our ability to show that some sentence comes out true on every truth-value assignment to its component parts *prove* its tautologous nature? In a certain sense one may answer "yes," since it now has become customary (in large part as a result of the *Tractatus*) to take this as a *definition* of "tautology."[31] But, of course, the real question here concerns the basis of this convention or, perhaps better, the implications of adopting it. Are we, in so doing, forced to regard tautologies as senseless, pseudo-propositions? It seems not. Indeed, it is quite common to take the truth table method as revealing tautologies to be truths that hold in "all possible worlds."[32] Far from showing the emptiness of such expressions, the Tractarian technique can be used to buttress an understanding of them as transcendent, "super truths." Given the possibility of a general decision procedure, the same could then be said of all the propositions of logic.

It may appear as if I am now suggesting that Wittgenstein is unwittingly attempting to prove the opposite of what he had intended about the nature of the logical proposition. But that is not the conclusion to be drawn here. Instead, the point is to see the independence of the question of the existence of a general decision procedure from the philosophical moral of the *Tractatus'* remarks; it is to start to bring out how uncomfortably the notion of proof fits in this context. This, I suggest, is precisely the force of the close of 6.126:

> We prove a logical proposition by creating it out of other logical propositions by applying in succession certain operations, which again generate tautologies out of the first. (And from a tautology only tautologies *follow*.)
> Naturally this way of showing that its propositions are tautologies is quite unessential to logic. Because the proposition, from which the proof starts, must show without proof that they are tautologies.

Similarly we find:

> Proof in logic is only a mechanical expedient to facilitate the recognition of tautology, where it is complicated. (TLP 6.1262)
> All propositions of logic are of equal rank; there are not some which are essentially primitive and others deduced from these.
> Every tautology itself shows that it is a tautology. (TLP 6.127)

Now, these remarks are difficult and must be treated carefully. It would be easy to suppose that this talk of tautologies showing themselves as such rests on the possibility of some special moment of insight, as if we might grasp via an act of intuition the tautological essence of the logical proposition. One might think that this would serve to explain why proof would be viewed as ultimately unnecessary in the case of recognizing tautologies. We have seen, though, that the notion of showing is never used in connection with any such conjectured psychological state. Wittgenstein in fact is explicit in his denial of the relevance of psychological states to the issues with which he is concerned. This is evident in his dismissal of the philosophical significance of psychology – "Psychology is no nearer related to philosophy, than is any other natural science" (TLP 4.1121) – but even more so at

5.552: "The 'experience' which we need to understand logic is not that such and such is the case, but that something *is;* but that is *no* experience." Invoking magical flashes of insight will be of no use to Wittgenstein (or to us) in clarifying how logical propositions can be said to show their tautologous nature.

I suggest instead that we view these remarks as reflections on what it means to call something a tautology. Wittgenstein says that one way to prove a proposition of logic is by generating it from other such propositions by the application of certain formal rules. Such a procedure is followed in the "old logic," as Wittgenstein calls it in "Notes Dictated to G. E. Moore in Norway"(NB 109) – that is, the formal systems of the *Principia* and *Begriffsschrift* (and *Grundgesetze*). His contention here, however, is not that this is an inadequate method of proof that is to be scrapped in favor of a generalized version of the truth table method. To be sure, the systems of Frege and Russell, with their reliance on axioms and rules of inference, are viewed as giving us a misleading conception of the nature of logic, as we shall discuss shortly. But their method fares no worse than the *Tractatus'* in terms of what it actually *proves* about the nature of the logical proposition: in either case, Wittgenstein is suggesting, all that is shown is that a given proposition "belongs to logic" (TLP 6.126) – that is, that it is of a certain form, that it can be grouped along side certain other linguistic signs.[33] While the truth table method may more clearly display the uniform character of a certain class of propositions, the real point is that this "mechanical expedient" does not, any more than an axiomatic method of proof, *tell us* what that character comes to; once more we see that it makes no sense to speak of proof in connection with the ascription of the term "tautology" to a proposition. Indeed, it would seem that we misunderstand the *Tractatus'* use of this term if we imagine it to refer to any sort of "property" that may or may not be found to belong to a proposition. For Wittgenstein, a tautology is instead part of what a particular linguistic form *is.* Such forms "show themselves" to be tautologies just because having this nature is bound up with the entire role that they play, with the way they function in our language.

This point can be made clearer through a consideration of the nature of the significant sentence's content. At 4.31 and 4.431, Wittgenstein shows how the proposition's "truth conditions" – what we have seen to be the sense of the proposition – can be set out in the now familiar form of a truth table. Thus the truth possibilities of the elementary propositions and various combinations of their resulting truth values are listed, and the truth functional nature of the molecular proposition made perspicuous. Now it is important to emphasize that, for Wittgenstein, the truth table can itself be construed as an expression. He remarks: "A proposition is the expression of agreement and disagreement with the truth-possibilities of the elementary propositions" (TLP 4.4). And at 4.431: "The proposition *is* the expression of its truth-conditions" (emphasis mine). If we standardize the ordering of the truth-possibilities of the elementary propositions in the truth tables, then "the last column is by itself an expression of the truth-conditions" (TLP 4.442) and constitutes a propositional sign. Of course, Wittgenstein must not be understood as thereby suggesting that "(TTFT) (p,q)" is the preferred expression, that it somehow constitutes what we *really* mean when we assert "p ⊃ q." On the contrary, his point here is just to bring out the deceptive nature of this demand for the "real sense" of a sentence. "(TTFT) (p,q)" and "p ⊃ q," he is suggesting, are equivalent expressions; the first can, for certain purposes or in certain contexts, simply replace the second.[34] But that means that the *philosopher's* interest in sense – the desire for a proper specification of *what* that sense is – cannot find its fulfillment in either of these expressions as such. This desire is instead satisfied by seeing what is common to these symbols and all others that could replace them; what "p" "really" says emerges just through the possibility of translating between equivalent means of expressing this same sense. The sense of "p" is, as Wittgenstein asserts at 4.022 and 4.461, only *shown.*

In the same way that the significant proposition shows its sense, then, the logical proposition can be said to show that it is a tautology. Wittgenstein explicitly draws the connection between these ideas at 4.461: "The proposition shows what it says, the tautology and the contradiction that they say nothing." We must, however, be clear on the nature of this analogy. For the point is not that being tautologous is, like the sense of a genuine proposition, that which the logical proposition says – the latter, since it is *sinnlos,* does not say anything. Instead, what the *Tractatus* is suggesting is that we stand in the same position when we ask for the sense of a proposition as when we ask why it is tautologous. Certainly, in both cases one can offer *some* sort of response to this question: to a confusion about p's sense we can, as

I have just been emphasizing, provide alternate ways of saying the same thing; similarly, we have seen that Wittgenstein holds open the possibility of a number of different methods of exposing tautologies (of what at 6.1263 he calls "proof[s] *in* logic"). But the key idea is that all such answers would seem to stand on the same level as what is questioned about.

It is in the acknowledgment of this point that we see the incoherence of asking for an ultimate justification for the ascription of "tautology," for some underlying something to which we can appeal. There is, one might say, nothing hidden from us, no new facts that need to be brought to light. Instead, Wittgenstein's real aim in this whole discussion is only to draw our attention to a difference of form: he is emphasizing how *unlike* the role of "p v ~p" is from that of "p v ~q" and, by terming the former a tautology, urging us to take that difference in a certain way. To grant this, however, is just to grant that the assertion about the tautologous nature of the proposition of logic, rather than being put forth as a self-standing claim, an attempt to offer an overarching characterization of logical truth, is as dialectical a move as any other in the *Tractatus.* It takes its significance precisely from the tendency to *assimilate* "p v ~p" and "p v ~q," the assimilation that Wittgenstein sees as lying at the heart of Frege and Russell's conception of logic as a science of maximally general truths. Shorn from the interplay with such a tendency, from the desire for insight into the world's essential nature that it bespeaks, the text's claims about tautology have no standing whatsoever.

What this suggests, in turn, is that the *Tractatus'* whole point in this context is contained in the details of its account of the propositions of logic, in its particular way of distinguishing such linguistic forms from significant utterances. One means the text has of drawing this distinction involves the possibility of what 6.126 calls "calculating the logical properties of the symbol." If we consider this phrase by itself, it is quite natural to suppose that Wittgenstein is here referring to something like a decision procedure.[35] But 6.126, like all of the remarks in the 6.1s, must be read in light of the *Tractatus'* discussion of the picture and its subsequent account of analysis. Let us look at this passage now in its entirety:

> Whether a proposition belongs to logic can be calculated by calculating the logical properties of the *symbol.*

> And this we do when we prove a logical proposition. For without troubling ourselves about a sense and a meaning, we form the logical propositions out of others by mere *symbolic rules* (*Zeichenregeln;* "rules dealing with signs").
> We prove a logical proposition by creating it out of other logical propositions by applying in succession certain operations, which again generate tautologies out of the first. (And from tautology only tautologies *follow.*)
> Naturally *this* way of showing that its propositions are tautologies is quite unessential to logic [emphasis mine]. Because the propositions, from which the proof starts, must show without proof that they are tautologies.

Notice, first, the structure of Wittgenstein's claims. He does not say that if anything is a proposition of logic, then it must be provable by logical properties of the symbol. On the contrary, he only speaks of what happens "*when* we prove a logical proposition." Rather than asserting something about what must be the case for every possible proposition of a certain form, as he would if he were relying on the idea of a general decision procedure, he is only concerned to describe what happens in those instances where a proof is available.

Any such proof, he suggests, will involve the recognition of a feature of the symbol.[36] Now, we recall that a symbol or expression for Wittgenstein is any part of a proposition that contributes to its sense and that it is properly presented by a variable. We saw that the symbol can serve as a way of showing what is common to a particular class of propositions and thus of characterizing the meanings of the names. In speaking at this juncture of a "property *of* the *symbol,*" Wittgenstein would then seem to have moved up a level – he is concerned with what is common to a *number* of classes of propositions.[37] Of course, since, as I have suggested, there is for Wittgenstein no logical hierarchy of variables, this higher order property will be signified simply by a variable (rather than by, say, a second order variable), just like the *Bedeutungen* of the names. Nonetheless, the possibility of recognizing such a property is significant. For it necessarily involves focusing on the use of the picture as a pictorial whole or fact – the ways that it can "represent," in the Tractarian sense of the term. We can refer to properties of symbols only when we ignore everything having to do with the inner constitution of some class of propositions (their particular logico-pictorial forms) and consider no more than what is common to their capacities to be projected across logical space – that is, what allows them to represent some particular state of affairs in the first place. The *Tractatus'* claim is then that proof of the logical proposition relies on this common element alone.

Certainly, this point is evident when we consider a proof via the use of a truth table: this device allows us to see clearly that the truth of, say, "p v ~p" can be determined with reference only to the truth possibilities of this propositional schema (its mode of projection). Unlike in the case of the significant proposition, we do not take into account the specific content of "p," but only how the proposition is constructed. The point can also be seen, however, by reflecting on the axiomatic style of proof characteristic of the Frege and Russell systems – in fact it is the latter that Wittgenstein appears to have chiefly in mind in this passage, as I implied above. For, according to Wittgenstein, proof in the *Principia* is simply a matter of demonstrating that one linguistic form can be generated out of another solely through the application of "rules dealing with signs." Here, too, it would seem, truth is determined just by showing how a proposition is constructed.

Given this way of construing the propositions of logic, the nature of their connection to reality begins to become clear. At 6.12, Wittgenstein puts it this way:

> The fact that the propositions of logic are tautologies *shows* the formal – logical – properties of language, of the world.
> That its constituent part connected together in this way give a tautology characterizes the logic of its constituent parts.
> In order that propositions connected together in a definite way may give a tautology they must have definite properties of structure. That they give a tautology when so connected shows therefore that they possess these properties of structure.

This passage suggests that Wittgenstein's point is not simply, as is often suggested, that genuine propositions state something, while the propositions of logic only show formal aspects of language and reality[38] (indeed, 4.121 makes clear that it is the genuine proposition that shows logical form). Rather, he says that the fact that the propositions of logic are *tautologies* is what shows those aspects. The *Sinnloskeit* of the logical proposition is then key: it is just through the disintegration of sense that results from the attempt to combine certain strings of signs into propositions that particular internal features of language/

reality come to the fore. As one might put it, to recognize a string of signs as a tautology is to recognize that that string is not *itself* attempting to say something, but only serving as a way of characterizing what a number of (genuine) propositions have in common. But this is to suggest that the propositions of logic are, for Wittgenstein, not propositions at all, but, as we implied above, variables – variables that reflect properties of the symbol. Such "propositions" can only show, since they ultimately constitute no more than certain means of describing an already given propositional class.

The full force of these considerations is then felt with the illustration that Wittgenstein provides at 6.1201: "That e.g. the proposition "*p*" and "~*p*" in the connexion "~(*p* & ~*p*)" give a tautology shows that they contradict one another. That the proposition "*p* ⊃ *q*," "*p*" and "*q*" connected together in the form "(*p* ⊃ *q*) & (*p*):⊃: (*q*)" give a tautology shows that *q* follows from *p* and *p* ⊃ *q*. That "(*x*).*fx*: ⊃ :*fa*" is a tautology shows that *fa* follows from (*x*).*fx*, etc. etc." What his examples bring out is that the internal features of language and reality with which he is here concerned, the properties of the symbol, are nothing other than what we normally think of as inferential connections *between* propositions. To say that, for example, "(p ⊃ q) v ~(p ⊃ q)" is a tautology is simply to describe a given class of propositions, to bring out a certain feature they have in common. And that, Wittgenstein is claiming, is all that we are doing when we say that "q" follows logically from "p" and "p ⊃ q."

This is precisely the view that is put forward in the *Notebooks:* "Logical propositions *are forms of proofs:* they shew that one or more propositions *follow* from one (or more)" (NB 109). The same point is made, albeit somewhat more obscurely, at 6.1264 of the *Tractatus:* "The significant proposition asserts something, and its proof shows that it is so; in logic every proposition is the form of a proof. Every proposition of logic is a modus ponens represented in signs. (And the modus ponens can not be expressed by a proposition)." The proposition of logic serves to, as it were, stamp some class of genuine propositions, to show how the members of that class share a particular form. We thus see even more clearly why, for Wittgenstein, the tautologousness of such propositions is regarded as basic. For this is simply to bring out that the proposition of logic serves as itself a way of characterizing, as a paradigm in this particular "language-game." Nothing can underlie the recognition of tautology because it is that very tautological nature that we rely on in describing the internal features of a given class of propositions.

Wittgenstein connects this point with the fact that "we often feel as though 'logical truths' must be *'postulated'* by us" (TLP 6.1223). This feeling reflects the recognition that the propositions of logic do not stand on their own, that they, in some sense, depend for their life on what *we* do. But Wittgenstein wants to bring out how it is nonetheless misleading to describe matters that way: "We can in fact postulate [the 'logical truths'] in so far as we can postulate an adequate notation" (TLP 6.1223). This same idea is elaborated on at 6.124:

> The logical propositions describe the scaffolding of the world, or rather they represent (*darstellen*) it. They presuppose that names have meaning (*Bedeutung*) and that elementary propositions have sense. And this is their connection with the world. It is clear that it must show something about the world that certain combinations of symbols – which essentially have a definite character – are tautologies. Herein lies the decisive point. We said that in the symbols which we use something is arbitrary, something not. In logic it is only the latter that expresses: but that means that logic is not a field in which *we* express what we wish with the help of signs, but rather one in which the nature of the absolutely necessary signs speaks for itself. If we know the logical syntax of any sign language, then we have already been given all the propositions of logic.

To say that logical propositions presuppose that names have meaning and that elementary propositions have sense is again to emphasize the primacy of a notation. It is to get us to see how the propositions of logic ride on the back of the genuine propositions and thus have no status apart from the latter. The logical proposition indeed reflects something about language and the world. But that is precisely because the values of this variable are propositions: in describing them we *ipso facto* describe something about the reality with which they are concerned. The connection of logic with the world is preserved, one might say, at the price of any interest in pointing it out.

Still, the *Tractatus'* account of the propositions of logic as tautologies is meant to do more than suggest that (what this text takes to be) the standard approach to logic – the Frege/Russell formalization of logical inference by means of axioms and so-called rules of inference – is merely uninteresting or superfluous. Instead, Wittgenstein is ultimately concerned to claim that the very attempt to engage in this sort of formalization is an indication of a deep confusion. What he understands to be the real motivation for such an enterprise is implicit in the above passage: it is the desire for *us* to specify the "nature of the absolutely necessary signs," rather than allowing the signs to "speak for themselves." How are we to understand such a desire? For Wittgenstein the point would seem to be, as always, that the philosophical logician imagines there to be a subject matter, an underlying structure, corresponding to what is necessary in the sign; on the *Tractatus'* account the logician imagines that in setting forth his formal language he has in fact laid bare that essential structure. In saying that the signs must speak for themselves, Wittgenstein is then suggesting how misleading is this notion of an underlying logical structure, how an understanding of logical inference is really only a matter of looking at the symbolism in the right way.[39] One is reminded here of 3.3411. After remarking that "the essential in a symbol [what is in the 6.1s referred to as the symbol's 'logical properties'] is that which all symbols which can fulfill the same purpose have in common" (TLP 3.341), Wittgenstein, as we recall, goes on: "One could therefore say the real name is that which all symbols, which signify an object, have in common" (TLP 3.3411). Once more it is evident that this "real name" is really no name at all:[40] Wittgenstein's account of the propositions of logic as tautologies is meant to show that the "entity" sought by the logician (that which is common to all the symbols) is ultimately nothing but a view of an entire linguistic *system*.

The above-quoted reference to the proposition of logic as "a modus ponens represented in signs" is meant to drive home very much the same idea. Here Wittgenstein specifically has in mind the notion of a "rule of inference" as it functions in the formal logic of Frege and Russell. The apparent need for such inference rules can easily be taken to imply that logic is concerned essentially to articulate the underlying relations between propositions – as if these rules provided the necessary *justification* for the transition from one proposition to another. Now earlier, at 5.132, Wittgenstein announces his rejection of any justificatory use of inference rules, remarking that they "are senseless (*sinnlos*) and would be superfluous." His position is thus often likened to Lewis Carroll's in his famous article about the "paradox" surrounding modus ponens. Carroll shows how the demand for a justification for the inference from "p" and "p ⊃ q" to "q" seems to require adding "(p & (p ⊃ q)) ⊃ q" as an additional premise in the inference; but by the same reasoning, the connection between this new premise and the original ones would also stand in need of justification, requiring a further premise, which then must itself be linked to the previous ones, and so on in infinite regress.[41] Certainly, insofar as Wittgenstein and Carroll are both concerned to draw our attention to the special status of rules of inference, there is a connection between their views. But while Carroll's argument may well lead us to conclude that there is some special sort of "immediate," unformalizable character to logical inference, the *Tractatus,* I suggest, is primarily concerned to shift our perspective so that we no longer feel any urge to account for *why,* for example, "q" follows from "p" and "p ⊃ q" in the first place.

Wittgenstein holds that we should understand "(p & (p ⊃ q)) ⊃ q" as a tautology; we are to see this string of signs as a *sinnlos* symbol that represents internal features of a class of propositions, which expresses what is common to them. But that should make apparent that there can be no question of justification or explanation in this context: it is not because some given set of propositions is a tautology that we say they have certain features in common but, rather, it is because they share those features that they are said to belong to the class of tautologies. Since those common features are what we ordinarily refer to as inferential relations, every proposition of logic can then be said to constitute a "modus ponens" (in an extended sense of the term) – a means of reflecting the space of logical relations that *already* are taken to obtain.

As always, logic for Wittgenstein comes in after the fact, as it were, as a way of describing an already given expanse of significant utterances. The confusion the *Tractatus* sees reflected in the logician's reliance on inference rules betokens a reversal of this priority. The logician imagines that he is in the position of legislating to language, that through his rules of inference he is giving *a priori* license to certain inference patterns. For the *Tractatus,* though, what he is trying to say here is expressed simply in our willingness to count *these* particular propositions as exemplifying a certain form, as an instance of that tautology. Rules of inference thus really constitute nothing more than a misguided attempt to specify *a priori* the range of certain variables – which is to say that Wittgenstein's criticism here has much the same form as his earlier criticism of the theory of types.[42] This explains why he ends 6.1264 with the parenthetical remark: "And the modus ponens [which every proposition of logic represents] cannot be expressed by a proposition." That is, Wittgenstein is suggesting that, just like the sort of type restrictions that Russell attempts to institute, the logical connection between the premises "p" and "p ⊃ q" and the conclusion "q" can only be shown – everything the philosopher would want to state here comes out in how we speak, in the way we operate with a set of propositions of this form.

V

We now can begin to see how these considerations tie in with Wittgenstein's remarks about the general form of the proposition. The latter notion is evidently meant to have tremendous significance in the *Tractatus:* it is given extensive treatment through the 5s and indeed constitutes the subject of one of the seven principle remarks of the book – remark 6. We note, then, that the concept of the general form of the proposition is first introduced following the *Tractatus'* initial discussion of tautology at 4.46–4.4661:

> Now it appears to be possible to give the most general form of proposition (*die allgemeinste Satzform*); i.e., to give a description of the propositions of some one sign language, so that every possible sense can be expressed by a symbol, which falls under the description, and so that every symbol which falls under the description can express a sense, if the meanings (*Bedeutungen*) of the names are chosen accordingly.
> It is clear that in the description of the most general form of proposition *only* what is essential to it may be described – otherwise it would not be the most general form.
> That there is a general form is proved by the fact that there cannot be a proposition whose form could not have been foreseen (i.e., constructed). The general form of proposition is: Such and such is the case. (TLP 4.5)

As we have seen, the tautology (or contradiction) is for Wittgenstein a means of showing what is common to certain classes of propositions and thereby of characterizing various internal features of language and the world. The general form of the proposition, as constituting what is essential to the proposition, can then be seen as a presentation of what is common to *all* propositions whatsoever. It is thus a kind of generalization of the tautology, giving us in the most abstract terms possible just the proposition's way of "representing" (again in the Tractarian sense of the term) the world. For this reason, Wittgenstein equates this general form with "the one logical constant" (TLP 5.47) and holds that its specification is "the essence of all description, therefore the essence of the world" (TLP 5.4711).

Still, if it is important to see that the possibility of specifying the general form of the proposition is continuous with the account of logic as tautologous, it is also important to be clear on how this possibility initially emerges out of the discussion of the picture. Once more, then, we recall that the original connection between the picture and reality is, for Wittgenstein, secured by the identity of their pictorial forms – which is to say by the fact that a picture, according to the *Tractatus'* way of using the term, is always a picture of the world. Given this background of a common form, we can speak of all the states of affairs that a picture can be used to depict, that is, of the existent and non-existent atomic facts that the picture "presents." The picture is then said to "represent" one possibility of its projection on to those states of affairs and thus a kind of choice within the field of what it presents. But that means that what the picture represents – the specific determination of reality that is thereby made – will always be a state of affairs that *could* obtain.[43] If we can then specify in general all the methods of projecting the picture on to reality, we will have described what is common to all states of affairs whatsoever – the essence of the world. Since Wittgenstein in fact insists on the *singleness* of the logical coordinate system through which that projection occurs, the necessity of its being given all at once and in its entirety, such a complete *a priori* characterization of the methods of representation should then be available. And that is precisely what is given by his specification of the general form of the proposition.[44]

At the same time, this very story helps to make evident the emptiness of the sort of summing up of the nature of logic allowed for by the *Tractatus.* For we note at once that this *a priori* account of representation can only be given by abstracting away from the form of the picture, from what allows it to present the existence and nonexistence of atomic facts. In more linguistic terms, this is just to say that the identification of the *general* form of the proposition necessitates ignoring the specific *logical* forms of the propositions that are characterized. But then the expression of the general form of the proposition must be a (high level) variable, as 4.53 explicitly states, bringing to the fore what is common to properties of the symbol. Thus, in 4.5, the passage quoted above, Wittgenstein says that all the symbols making up that expression are guaranteed to have a sense, as long as "the meanings of the names are chosen accordingly." Since it is only when the names in a linguistic string *actually* designate meanings (i.e., logical forms) that a genuine proposition is given, this suggests that, as it stands, the expression for the general propositional form can be no more than a possibility for a proposition, a kind of bare container in which a content is to be placed.[45] Wittgenstein's paraphrase of the general form of the proposition as "Such and such is the case" is thus not, as Fogelin implies,[46] meant to communicate a significant result. Rather, in the transparent vacuity of this culminating statement we are meant to see the vacuity of the Frege/Russell logic, of any attempt to specify *a priori* the limits of thought and language. Wittgenstein, in other words, is here once more giving expression to the thought that animates the whole *Tractatus:* namely, that to the extent that we can gain clarity about the nature of our real aim in logic and philosophy, we will see that this aim has lost its allure.[47]

We must be clear on how this deflationary view of the task of philosophy is also connected with the previously discussed notion of logical analysis. In this regard, the above mentioned distinction between "general form" and "logical form" is crucial. The logical forms, as we have seen, are equated with the meanings of the names of the elementary propositions. The possibility of giving some sort of specification of the logical forms – that is, the possibility of a complete analysis into elementary propositions – is secured by what Wittgenstein calls the definiteness of sense, the acknowledgment that the possible ascriptions that may be made to reality cannot await our discovery (the same thought that, as we have seen, lies behind the "argument for simples" in the opening section of the text). We saw from the discussion in the 3s, however, that such a specification could only emerge through a consideration of the proposition as it is used (of what *I* mean in some context) – it cannot be given in advance. This point is in fact reaffirmed several times toward the end of the 5s:

> We must now answer *a priori* the question as to all possible forms of the elementary propositions.
> The elementary proposition consists of names. Since we cannot give the number of names with different meanings, we cannot give the composition of the elementary propositions. (TLP 5.55)
> The enumeration of any special forms would be entirely arbitrary. (TLP 5.554)

> It is clear that we have a concept of the elementary proposition apart from its special logical form.
> Where, however, we can build symbols according to a system, there this system is the logically important thing and not the single symbols.
> And how would it be possible that I should have to deal with forms in logic which I can invent: but I must have to deal with that which makes it possible for me to invent them. (TLP 5.555)
> There cannot be a hierarchy of the forms of the elementary propositions. Only that which we ourselves construct can we foresee.
> The *application* (*Anwendung*) of logic decides what elementary propositions there are.
> What lies in its application logic cannot anticipate. (TLP 5.557)
> If I cannot give elementary propositions *a priori* then it must lead to obvious nonsense to try to give them. (TLP 5.5571)

The actual carrying out of the analysis into elementary propositions is thus not itself part of "logic," as Wittgenstein understands it in the *Tractatus*. Nonetheless, the *possibility* of such an analysis is crucial. First, as we have seen, reflection on what it would have to entail is important in revealing the emptiness of the philosopher's attempt to get at the fundamental categories of thought and language – the specification of *what* the world, at its core, must be like. Second, the imagined results of this analysis figure in Wittgenstein's summing up of that which *can* be stated in advance – namely, the general form of the proposition. For, as we shall discuss in some detail in a moment, the more technical presentation of that general propositional form involves conceiving of all propositions as truth functions of the elementary propositions; to be able to present the domain of the *a priori* in its entirety, we must be able to conceive of the fundamental logical forms as, in some sense, given.[48]

One might say, then, that the notion of a complete analysis ultimately serves as a kind of thought experiment for gaining clarity about the technical logic developed by Frege and Russell, for bringing out how the possibility of the latter rests on our *already* having a handle on the meaningful content of our language. As Wittgenstein puts the point at 5.552: "Logic *precedes* every experience – that something is *so*. It is before the How, not before the What." We have seen that, for the *Tractatus*, the "what" – the content of our language – is not given independently of the logical scaffolding; in this sense logic precedes every experience. But at the same time, Wittgenstein is suggesting that logic has no life *apart from* the sensical expanse with which we are presented; his real point is then that the formalisms of Frege and Russell constitute no more than an account of our *way* of constructing the proposition, our manner of projecting our linguistic forms on to reality.

Nonetheless, one might well wonder just how "deflationary" Wittgenstein's conception of this whole enterprise really is. While it may be granted that it challenges the Frege/Russell picture of a determinate logical content, we hardly seem to be left with nothing to replace that picture. On the contrary, as the above passage suggests, the *Tractatus* would in the end appear to present a quite Kantian[49] view of logic as a condition of the possibility of all experience. To be sure, just as with Kant's transcendental conditions of knowledge (the forms of the intuition and the categories of the understanding), a prior given, a "what" on which to operate, is required – thus logic can be said to determine only "how" the world is represented. But why would that entail the emptiness of the specification of logic – that is, of the Tractarian analogue to Kant's transcendental theorizing? Kant, after all, draws no such a conclusion about the status of his own work. Indeed, Wittgenstein would seem to have done Kant one better, since his version of transcendental logic is apparently capable of precise, purely formal expression. The *Tractatus'* conclusion may be a step back from the metaphysical excesses of Frege and Russell, but it ultimately does not constitute a complete undermining of their respective enterprises.

Or so one might argue. Now the general direction of (what I claim to be) Wittgenstein's response should, I hope, at this point be at once apparent: his central idea is that the very possibility of formal expression of the general form of the proposition itself shows the emptiness of his "transcendental philosophy."[50] Nonetheless, I do not view the above as a mere straw man objection, as it points to the need for understanding in more detail Wittgenstein's formal specification of the general propositional form. *How* it is that $[(\text{i.e, } \bar{p}, \bar{\xi}, N(\bar{\xi}))]$ is meant to say no more than "Such and such is the case"?

To answer this question, and thus to conclude this part of our discussion of the *Tractatus*, we must first consider Wittgenstein's notion of an operation. This term is introduced at 5.21: "We can bring out these internal relations [between the structures of propositions] in our manner of expression, by presenting a proposition as the result of an operation which produced it from other propositions (the bases of the operation)." He then continues:

> The internal relation which orders a series [of forms] is equivalent to the operation by which one term arises from another. (TLP 5.232)
> Truth-functions of elementary propositions are results of operations with elementary propositions as bases. (These operations I call truth-operations.) (TLP 5.234)
> The sense of a truth-function of *p* is a function of the sense of *p*.
> Negation, logical addition, logical multiplication, etc. etc. are operations. (Negation reverses the sense of a proposition). (TLP 5.2341)

The operation is, in the first instance, Wittgenstein's formal means of handling the truth functional connectives. Given our previous discussion of the *Tractatus'* treatment of this issue, what is said here about the operation should then not come as a surprise. As giving prominence to the representing dimension of the picture, the operation will describe a common feature of a class of symbols – thus Wittgenstein says that it brings out internal relations between the structures of propositions. For the same reason, he remarks that "the occurrence of an operation does not characterize the sense of a proposition" (TLP 5.25): this is just to reiterate the point that the expression of a common feature of a class of symbols will abstract from the logical forms of the propositions characterized, that the logical constants are only applied to propositions already *having* a sense.[51] (Wittgenstein is of course not here asserting that the truth-operations have no effect whatsoever on the sense of a proposition; after all, he expressly holds above that that sense is reversed by negation. Instead, what he is saying, as always in the *Tractatus,* is that logic assumes a pregiven content in a certain sense, that, as an operation, it does not touch the internal make-up of the proposition.) Similarly, too, he insists that the notions of operation and function must not be confused with one another (TLP 5.25). Although both the propositional function – that is, the symbol – and the operation – the reworking of the truth-function – are, for Wittgenstein, expressed by means of a variable (this is explicitly stated of the operation at 5.24 and 5.2522), they stand, as we have seen, at different levels. Hence, as 5.251 emphasizes, the function cannot be its own argument ("x is a table is a table" does not characterize any class of propositions), while the operation can take one of its own results as its base (~p can again be denied).[52]

Wittgenstein gives his more formal presentation of the notion of an operation at 5.2522:

> The general term of the formal series *a, O'a, O'O'a,* . . . I write thus: "[*a, x, O'x*]." This expression in brackets is a variable. The first term of the expression is the beginning of the formal series, the second the form of an arbitrary term x of the series, and the third the form of that term of the series which immediately follows x.

This makes it evident that, for the *Tractatus,* the characterization by means of an operation involves a recursive specification: in the variable contained in the brackets, "a" represents the basis step, "x" the nth step in the development of the series, and "O'x" (the application of the operation to the nth step) the nth + 1 step. To see how Wittgenstein will make use of such a specification, we must first understand the particular operation he is concerned to define – "N($\bar{\zeta}$)." "ξ," it is clear, is a Tractarian variable, a schema for one or more propositions. As we shall soon see, however, there is a question about how exactly to understand the functioning of the "$\bar{\zeta}$" notation. But as that question becomes most relevant in connection with the account of quantification, we can for the moment ignore it and simply follow Wittgenstein's instructions at 5.501 to take the "$\bar{\zeta}$" as standing for all the values of a given variable. "N($\bar{\zeta}$)" is then to be understood as "the negation of all the values of the propositional variable ξ" (TLP 5.502); it constitutes a generalized version of the Sheffer stroke of joint denial.

Confining ourselves for the time being to the context of truth functional logic, it is not difficult to see what Wittgenstein has in mind. For example, substituting "p" and "q" (which can stand for either elementary or nonelementary sentences) for "ξ," "N(p, q)" yields "~p & ~q," "N(N(p, q))" yields "~(~p & ~q) & ~(~p & ~q)," i.e. "p v q," and so on. The variable represented at 6-[($\bar{p}$, $\bar{\zeta}$, N $\bar{\zeta}$)] – then provides for the possibility of making such selections from the set of all elementary propositions. In this way, Wittgenstein can hold that he has characterized the whole of truth-functional logic: since the Sheffer stroke constitutes a truth-functionally complete set, every nonquantificationally complex sentence would appear somewhere in the formal series generated by iterated applications of the N operator to the elementary propositions.

Just this need for *iterated* applications of operator N is key in assessing the import of this approach. For what Wittgenstein is here seeking to bring out is what has been implicit throughout the *Tractatus* – namely, that any systematic presentation of logic must rely on the "etc.," the "and so on."[53] Indeed, he expressly remarks: "The concept of the successive application of an operation is equivalent to the concept 'and so on' " (TLP 5.2523).[54] The point, in other words, is that the "givenness" of the whole of logical space – that is, of that which the picture was said to "present" – is ultimately just the possibility of our always being able to go on, to continue a pattern. Certainly, our ability to identify such a pattern is important, in that it allows for the possibility of, as Wittgenstein puts it in the *Notebooks*, "constructing logic and mathematics . . . [55] from the fundamental laws and primitive signs" (NB 89). (Conversely, we might note, precisely the absence of this sort of pattern precludes an *a priori* specification of the forms of the elementary propositions; one could say that there is simply no explanation of *why* it is nonsense to speak of the weight of a noise.)[56] But the force of Wittgenstein's own characterization of the general form of the proposition is to make apparent that logic is *no more* than that – that, in the end, the domain of the *a priori* is nothing but the possibility[57] of repeated applications of a rule.

Still, even if we accept this as an interpretation of Wittgenstein's analysis of truth functional logic, it is not at once apparent how this same sort of treatment could be extended to quantificational formulas. For consider how generality is expressed in the notation supplied by the *Tractatus*. As that notation includes no sign for the quantifier, Wittgenstein must rely on the possibility of applying the N operator to a potentially infinite number of propositional arguments. Thus 5.52 reads: "If the values of ξ are the total values of a function *fx* for all values of *x*, then $N(\bar{\xi}) = \sim(\exists x)fx$" (TLP 5.52). In other words, if the values of the function "fx" are the propositions "fa," "fb," "fc," . . . then "N(fx)" is equivalent to the joint denial of all those propositions, that is, to "~fa & ~fb & ~fc, . . . ," an expression that is equivalent to "∀x~fx." A further application of N would then yield the formula "∃xfx," and so on. In this way, Wittgenstein's N operator is capable of handling generality[58] and in a manner that is seemingly consistent with his truth-operational understanding of the proposition.

The central question that this approach raises, however, concerns the original specification of the values of the variable to which N is applied.[59] For what does it mean to say that a propositional variable "gives us" a set of values? If the notion of an operation is needed to clarify the givenness that belongs to the infinite expanse of logical space, how can the givenness of a potentially infinite set of propositions be here treated as unproblematic? Moreover, such a view would commit Wittgenstein to understanding generality in terms of logical sum or product: to treat the variable as a name for a very lengthy list of propositional values is just to take a universally quantified statement as nothing but a (possibly infinitely) long conjunction. But the *Tractatus* asserts that the concept "all" must be *"disassociated from"* the truth-functions and explicitly criticizes Frege and Russell for "introduc[ing] generality in connexion with the logical product or the logical sum" (TLP 5.521).

One might suppose these difficulties can be circumvented by supposing that, since a variable is understood as an indication of a type of proposition, it is imagined somehow to specify its values *as* a set, as a kind of totality. Wittgenstein's point would then be that in denying this variable we simultaneously deny all its values, without having to enumerate these one by one.[60] This could seem to be why he distinguishes generality from logical sum or product. While this interpretation is not altogether incorrect (as we shall see), the problem is that in requiring that the N operator be applied directly to the propositional variable in this way, we run up against the earlier claim prohibiting the operation from characterizing a sense. For N in this case effectively serves as a quantifier binding a free variable and thus would now be responsible for turning an open sentence into a genuine proposition.

Wittgenstein's understanding of generality cannot then involve such an approach. To see what he has in mind instead, we first must look at 5.522: "That which is peculiar to the 'symbolism for generality' is, firstly, that it refers to a logical proto-picture (*logisches Urbild;* Ogden "prototype"), and secondly that it makes constants prominent." This rather dark remark becomes helpful when read in connection with Wittgenstein's earlier discussion of analysis. We thus recall his discussion of the complex at 3.24 and its connection with the account of the vagueness of the ordinary (unanalyzed) proposition. Rather than viewing the complex as a special kind of object on whose existence the meaningfulness of certain propositions depends, the *Tractatus,* as we saw, understands this notion linguistically – that is, as one or more logical forms or proto-pictures that have been contracted into an apparent name via definition. The proto-picture here functions as a means of *leaving room* for the things in the world to have a range of, say, color values, without our having to specify which value must be assumed. The complexity of the world is in this way reflected in a certain indeterminateness in the unanalyzed proposition. But then since the discussion at this point is intimately connected with generality (we recall 3.24's remark – echoing 5.522 – about how the "notation for generality contains a proto-picture"), it appears that it is precisely through this indeterminateness that we gain our understanding of the quantifier. Generality, in other words, is to be equated with the propositional constituent seen as a representative of an *arbitrary* location within a particular logical form.

What this discussion first makes apparent is that generality for Wittgenstein finds its natural home within the context of the significant (unanalyzed) proposition. After all, we saw earlier that the indeterminateness that marks the appearance of the logical proto-picture is understood as making possible just the *definiteness* of sense. In remarking that the symbolism for generality refers to a logical proto-picture, Wittgenstein is then not faced with Russell's problem about the status of an asserted propositional function.[61] He is not, in other words, led into viewing such a function as a genuine, self-standing proposition with a special sort of ambiguous sense. For him, instead, the application of the proto-picture is given just by its contribution to the sense of the proposition in which it occurs; generality, we might say, is absorbed into our means of representing the particularities of the world.

Still, even if Wittgenstein's account is not saddled with the notion of a propositional function as a self-standing assertion, one might still wonder if his reliance on the idea of a representative of an arbitrary formal place is any clearer than Russell's "ambiguous denoting." Here it becomes important to consider the above remark about the prominence of constants in the notation for generality. Now one might suppose that by "constants" Wittgenstein is thinking of "names" as opposed to "functions," but in fact at 3.312 he uses the term in almost the opposite sense: "[An expression] is therefore represented by the general form of the propositions which it characterizes. And in this form the expression is *constant* and everything else *variable.*" With this in mind, his point would then seem to be that generality brings into prominence what is common to a class of propositions, and that it does so precisely by taking certain parts of these propositions to be "variable," arbitrary. For Wittgenstein, then, the possibility of speaking of "all" assumes not the existence of a kind of indefinite entity, but a way of gesturing toward a symbol, a feature of the proposition that helps characterize its sense. In terms of the picture theory, we could say that generality requires us to pay attention to the internal structure of the picture – that is, to that which makes it into a picture in the first place.[62] In this way the quantifier is distinguished ("disassociated") from the truth functions, which, as we have seen, ignore the picture's internal makeup and concern only its projection as a whole.

It is by reflection on this idea that we begin to see the key to Wittgenstein's view of generality: the arbitrariness that is essential to a generalization is, it seems, equivalent just to the possibility of constructing a picture of a particular form. To illustrate, let us revert to our earlier example of the assertion "The watch is on the table." For the *Tractatus,* both the concept "watch" and the concept "on the table" are understood as here presenting implicit generalizations, but let us focus on the latter. How is the generality in the notion of something's being on the table to be expressed? Wittgenstein would suggest that it is evident precisely in the fact that I can understand this as saying "ϕ is at location a or ϕ is at b or ϕ is at c, and so on." The "and so on" here does not denote the "dots of laziness"; it is not as if my sentence constitutes an abbreviation for a lengthy disjunction that I really intend. But neither does that sentence present me with a rule for continuing this formal series, as in the case of the truth operations. Rather, the possibility of continuing this series is given just by a logico-pictorial form. To understand the form "on the table" is to see it as permitting this location or this location or . . . ; while I cannot list all the possible locations,[63] still I do not *happen on* a place for this watch that I did not anticipate. (Recall once more Wittgenstein's insistence that I know what I mean, that I do not discover the sense of my utterances.) The potentially infinite set of propositional values that is "given" by a Tractarian variable is here really just the possibility of placing the watch in any location allowed for by this particular form.

We now can begin to make better sense of the *Tractatus'* formal way of handling generality. This requires that we return to the difficulty that we earlier passed over – namely, the interpretation of "$\bar{\xi}$." Let us look more closely at 5.501, where the bar notation is introduced:

> An expression in brackets whose terms are propositions I indicate – if the order of the terms in the bracket is indifferent – by a sign of the

> form "$(\bar{\zeta})$." "ξ" is a variable whose values are the terms of the expression in brackets, and the line over the variable indicates that it is the representative of (*vertritt*) all its values in the brackets.

The problem here is that, since a variable for Wittgenstein serves to characterize a particular class of propositions (a point that is reiterated at 5.501), it is not at once obvious what is the difference between "ξ" and "$\bar{\xi}$." Wouldn't "ξ" be "representative of all its values" – would it not demarcate a whole class of propositions – *before* the bar has been added? We must then look at this issue in light of the above discussion. Given what we have seen to be Wittgenstein's understanding of generality, it would appear that what is in fact needed is to add to the expression of a propositional variable a means of specifying some arbitrary *member* or *members* of the class of propositions that it describes. This, I suggest, is precisely the function of the bar notation: to place the bar over "ξ" is to allow for the possibility of this variable[64] *standing in for*[65] some one or more of its values.[66] Wittgenstein's notation thus bring out how the possibility of a generalization does not require the occurrence of a free variable, how it involves only a means of alluding to a series of propositions of a given form.[67]

It now becomes clear how we are to understand the application of the N operator to a propositional function "fx." By means of the bar notation we are presented with the series of "fx's" values – "fa," "fb," "fc," . . . – and it is to those values that N is directly applied. It is then true, as we suggested above, that the result of this operation can be represented as "~fa & ~fb & ~fc,. . . ."[68] This is not meant to imply, however, that the application of N requires us actually to complete a (possibly infinitely) long enumeration, as Fogelin, for example, appears to hold.[69] For, again, 5.521 insists that generality must not be introduced in connection with logical sum or product; in the terms of the later Wittgenstein, we could say that the grammar of "infinite list" is entirely different from that of "enumeration." For the *Tractatus*, then, the ellipsis here represents just our capacity to designate any arbitrary sentence of this particular form (whatever form the variable schema "fx" is standing in for in some propositional context). We arrive at the generalization "∀x~fx," in other words, precisely through the *possibility* of our going on with the series "fa, fb, fc,. . . ." Given the possibility of unlimited applications of the N operator – as well as some means of marking scope distinctions – we can then in the same way generate every sentence of first-order logic.

The *Tractatus* thus can succeed in its task of showing how every proposition is the result of truth-operations on the elementary propositions. On this account, the generalization does not constitute a special kind of representation of the world, but simply a different way of applying a symbol. Thus, 5.526 emphasizes the potential equivalence of a purely generalized description to description by means of names: "One can describe the world completely by completely generalized propositions, i.e. without from the outset co-ordinating any name with a definite object. In order then to arrive at the customary way of expression we need simply say after an expression "there is one and only one *x*, which . . .": and this *x* is *a*." Rather than requiring the existence of special sorts of general facts, the possibility of forming general propositions rests once more on the possibility of continuing a pattern.

The notion of continuing a pattern thus plays a central, ineliminable role in the *Tractatus'* account. This may seem unsettling: one feels as if Wittgenstein's specification of the general form of the proposition has not truly gathered together, as it were, all the significant propositions – that we, at best, are only shown what it *would* mean to make a significant utterance in some given case. But that, of course, is just the point; that is what it is to say that we can give in advance no more than a *method* for representing the world.

The *Tractatus'* presentation of the general propositional form tells us that we know how to construct truth functions and sentences of unlimited quantificational complexity. To acknowledge that as the answer to the fundamental question of the philosophical or logical inquiry would seem to be to acknowledge the hollowness at that inquiry's heart. Wittgenstein suggests that it is with this answer that we must rest.

CHAPTER IV

THE LIBERATING WORD

I

Having completed our study of the details of the *Tractatus,* we can now reconsider from a more general perspective its fundamental aim or aims. There is, to be sure, a certain oddness in speaking here of a "conclusion," given what has been maintained thus far about the nature of this text; one wonders about the *status* of any summary remarks that we might have to offer. After all, if, as we have held throughout, a genuine understanding of the views of Wittgenstein can only be conveyed through a detailed appreciation of the movement of his thought, should we not suppose that everything of importance has already been said? Still, the question of how the author understands the ultimate outcome of his endeavor remains to be directly addressed. How *can* it be that the *Tractatus'* real purpose is an ethical one, as Wittgenstein suggests?

Before approaching the question, we would do well to review where we have been. We recall, then, that this text can be understood as, from the beginning, seeking to adopt a "logical" perspective on the world, the perspective from which the possibility of the facts is revealed. This involves the attempt to specify the real nature – the form – of the objects conditioning what is the case. We saw that this form, as given by the full range of the object's occurrences in a space of atomic facts, cannot be conceived as a self-standing entity, let alone as a further fact about the world. Instead, it is just a particular *way* of looking at what is the case: the revealing of the form of the object turns out to involve nothing more than a description of the world that will make perspicuous the combinatorial capacities of that description's fundamental components. While this move already shifts our understanding of the philosophical or logical inquiry, the real force of the *Tractatus'* claims here only begins to become apparent in the discussion of the picture. We saw, then, how the "picture theory" reinterprets that inquiry's central question as the demand for an *a priori* specification of the *possibility* of the positive/negative fact, what the *Tractatus* calls the picture's pictorial form (*Form der Abbildung*). The initial discussion of the picture brings us to see that any insight into the possibility of constructing a picture that can depict the world is parasitic on an understanding of the nonarbitrary aspect of the correlation of pictorial elements and their real-world counterparts (the analogue in this context to the form of the object). That such a correlation has been effected is assured simply by virtue of a particular fact's being a picture, but this possibility, according to Wittgenstein, cannot itself be represented, only shown. To say that, however, is just to express the emptiness of the question motivating this whole inquiry; it is to suggest that everything philosophy would want to say about the essence of representation emerges only through the application of the picture to the world.

We then saw how the treatment of picturing is extended to the notion of the proposition via the *Tractatus'* concepts of logical form and analysis. While, for Wittgenstein, the proposition is viewed as having a definite sense that it is the task of analysis to bring to light, it became apparent that this is not to be understood as an application to ordinary language of a Fregean refusal to countenance vague predicates. Rather, the assertion of definiteness of sense is equivalent to the denial of the possibility that I could *discover* what I mean, that logical analysis is required to reveal what my assertion really says. The ordinary proposition stands in perfect logical order and can do so precisely because it implicitly makes use of "proto-pictures" – that is, variables – that enable us to *allow for* a certain indeterminateness in our utterances. Analysis will then involve the attempt to delineate the occurrence of those variables and thereby make perspicuous the meanings (*Bedeutungen*) of the names. But since for the *Tractatus* having a variable entails already being given its (propositional) values, the variable's "delineation" comes to no more than the specification of a particular class of propositions. The meanings of the names emerge in what is common to that class – which implies that those meanings are not things or entities in the ordinary sense, but logical forms. The logical forms, in turn, are to be construed simply as ways of characterizing the already given expanse of significant utterances. What reflection on the idea of analysis thus makes clear is that, just as in the case of the picture and its form of representation, philosophy's proper concern – the *possibility* of making sense – is not a self-subsistent domain conditioning thought and language, but just a way of viewing how we in fact speak.

In Chapter III, we explored how the picture theory also underlies Wittgenstein's treatment of the logic of Russell's *Principia Mathematica* and Frege's *Begriffsschrift* and *Grundgesetze.* The picture, on the one hand, "presents" (*vorstellen*) all those states of affairs (both existent and nonexistent) it can be used to depict. On the other hand, it "represents" (*darstellen*) a particular state of affairs within that determinate space; Wittgenstein thus introduces his view of the logical constants as the specific methods by which the pictorial fact can be projected on to reality. We saw that the tautology (or contradiction) can be conceived as a means of bringing to the fore what is common to the specific methods of projection of a class of sentences, and hence as a way of characterizing (what we would ordinarily think of as) inferential connections between propositions. But since, for Wittgenstein, we can speak of what is common to any manner of representing the world whatsoever, it must also be possible to give the "general form" of the proposition. A kind of generalization of the tautology, this complete *a priori* characterization of the nature of depiction is summed up by Wittgenstein's generalized version of the Sheffer stroke, his operator N. We saw, however, how this presentation of the general form of the proposition relies on an ineliminable use of the ellipsis and thus does not constitute a genuine definition. Instead, it merely points us toward the possibility of continuing a pattern, of going on in the same way. Thus, the *Tractatus'* complete *a priori* characterization actually brings out the emptiness of the Fregean and Russellian view of logical inference. Far from dictating to thought its fundamental laws, we are meant to see that the formalisms of the *Begriffsschrift* and the *Principia* serve only to reflect the hollow casing in which the significant proposition is to be placed.

II

The *Tractatus'* discussion of the general form of the proposition is an appropriate place to begin our final reflections on the overall purpose of Wittgenstein's text. That discussion brings out, as we have just noted, how the simple possibility of following a rule lies at the heart of formal logic, of our grasp of the generality of its application. Now, in the Introduction to this study and at the end of the last chapter, we suggested that Wittgenstein's account must itself in a certain sense rely on our ability to continue a pattern that has been initiated. After all, the *Tractatus* does not attempt – nor *could* it attempt – to unravel one by one every confusion by which philosophy has been bedeviled. Instead, as we have emphasized, Wittgenstein seeks to carry out this task in a wholesale manner, through a clarification of the *essence* of those confusions. This entails, ultimately, that we grasp how to extend the kind of point the *Tractatus* makes to *any* (arbitrary) philosophical "problem" that should happen to grip us, that we are able to understand such a problem as a confusion, say, of formal and genuine concepts (to use just one of the formulations Wittgenstein employs). For the *Tractatus* to claim to have exposed the emptiness of philosophy *tout court,* we must be able to go on *in the same way* with the inquiry represented in the text.

But now we must face up to an important dissimilarity between the role of the "and so on" in the characterization of the significant proposition and its role in continuing the central philosophical task of the text as a whole. This difference is evident in the absence of any specification for the nonsensical pseudo-proposition corresponding to the "general form" of the (significant) proposition – in the absence, that is, of a systematic summing-up of what is common to all those utterances that Wittgenstein would describe as "nonsensical." And indeed, on reflection we realize that it would be contrary to the *Tractatus'* fundamental stance – its eschewal of general criteria of sense and nonsense, its reliance on a dialectical methodology – to attempt to provide any such general description of the pseudo-proposition. To paraphrase Tolstoy, one might say that for the *Tractatus* all significant sentences are alike,[1] while every nonsense utterance is nonsensical in its own way. There is and can be no logic of nonsense.

Of course, this is largely a reformulation of the point emphasized throughout regarding the absence of genuine arguments in the *Trac-*

tatus, the inability of Wittgenstein's text to *compel* us to adopt its perspective on the nature of philosophy. But now it appears as if this idea stands in fundamental tension with the text's aim of silencing altogether the philosophical voice. For without the capacity to indicate the common component – or components – of the nonsensical pseudo-proposition, what sense can there be in supposing that we might continue "in the same way" Wittgenstein's endeavor? What *is* the endeavor we are to continue?

One might be tempted to say that it is just on this dilemma that the early Wittgenstein's whole inquiry founders. But while we have emphasized throughout how there is indeed a shift in his later thought toward the recognition of the multifariousness of philosophical inquiry, it would be a mistake to suppose that Wittgenstein in the *Tractatus* has no response whatsoever to the question we are raising.[2] On the contrary, I suggest that his response is quite connected with his understanding of the point of the text as ultimately ethical. It is in ethical terms that the inquiry of the *Tractatus* can be said to assume a unity.

We may approach this issue by first reminding ourselves of the peculiar character of the dialectic in which this text is engaged. Over and over we have seen how Wittgenstein's key claims – his remarks about the nature of objects and the distinction between *Tatsache* and *Sachverhalte,* the characterization of logical truths as tautologies, the show/say distinction, and so on – can only be understood as responses to certain philosophical questions, indeed as the means of clarifying just what those questions are. We have stressed how this recognition precludes our taking Wittgenstein's remarks as general, self-standing claims, how, for him, there can be no purpose, no interest whatsoever in simply "asserting" that a logical truth is a tautology, or that certain features of the proposition can only be shown. Instead, these remarks serve their clarificatory purpose – they *become* "nonsense" in the requisite sense – only when they are taken in connection with, or as directed against, the metaphysical impulse they aim to eliminate. The inseparability of Wittgenstein and his metaphysical interlocutor is at the heart of the Tractarian dialectic.

One then thinks back again to the Preface and Wittgenstein's remark that his book will only be understood by those who have had the same or similar *Gedanken.* We are once more reminded of 6.54 as well, but now with a slightly different emphasis: he who *understands* me understands my propositions as nonsense. To grasp the propositions of the *Tractatus* is, it would seem, really to engage in a double movement. We are to see in them the kind of thing we ourselves are aiming for and simultaneously to recognize that aim as not achievable. We are to acknowledge as illusion what we thought was our sought-after end.[3] But then that is to say that the recognition of the nonsensicality of philosophy is, for Wittgenstein, always a recognition that we are at odds with *ourselves.*[4] Philosophical nonsense results not because of anything inherently unachievable but because of an ongoing conflict in our own desires and aims.[5] The true insight into nonsense, in turn, can then be nothing but a release from self-conflict, from this fundamental disharmony in our being. In liberating us from the inner discord that defines the metaphysical impulse, the *Tractatus* aims to deliver us to the world.

We might put matters as follows. To be in the grip of philosophical perplexity, for Wittgenstein, is not to be in a situation where one is incapable of finding a solution to a complex problem. Instead, the genuinely philosophical "problem" only appears as such to one who places certain demands on the world, on language, who insists that our understanding must conform to *this* model. Wittgenstein's aim, then, is to get us to see these demands as illegitimate, as an attempt to put our words to a task to which they are not suited; his aim is to bring us to acknowledge that our expectations for a philosophical explanation are in the end only *our* expectations. Hence his oft-quoted remark:

> Most propositions and questions that have been written about philosophical matters are not false but nonsensical. Consequently we cannot give any answer to questions of this kind, but can only point out that they are nonsensical. Most questions and propositions of philosophers arise from our failure to understand the logic of our language.
> (They are of the same kind as the question whether the good is more or less identical than the beautiful.)
> And it is not surprising that the deepest problems are in fact *not* problems at all. (TLP 4.003)

To say that the deepest problems are not problems at all is not, however, to trivialize philosophical perplexity, to sneer at those who are in its grip.[6] What the above remark refers to as the *depth* of philosophical (pseudo-) problems is taken seriously: for Wittgenstein, the impulse toward philosophy arises out of a sense of profound rupture with the world,[7] a sense that, as he puts it in the *Notebooks*,[8] "even if all *possible* scientific questions are answered *our problem is still not touched at all*" (NB 51).[9] Of course, this is a sense that is not peculiar to philosophers, but, on his view, one that is apt to be experienced by anyone we should regard as serious.[10] What Wittgenstein considers as characteristic of the philosophical approach, however, is just its tendency to misinterpret that feeling of disquiet, to misconstrue what is appropriate as a response. Our unease in the world crystallizes into unresolvable philosophical perplexity.

This whole issue can be seen to underlie the following important remarks:

> At the basis of the whole modern view of the world lies the illusion that the so-called laws of nature are the explanations of natural phenomena. (TLP 6.371)
>
> So people stop short at natural laws as at something unassailable, as did the ancients at God and Fate.
>
> And they both are right and wrong. But the ancients were clearer, in so far as they recognized one clear terminus, whereas the modern system makes it appear as though *everything* were explained. (TLP 6.372)

Wittgenstein claims that at the basis of the modern view is an "illusion." He is not suggesting, then, that the pursuit of philosophy is to be replaced by a kind of scientism, a belief that the deepest yearnings of human beings can finally be met in the context of scientific progress. But neither are we to turn to nonscientific modes of explanation. The ancients are here commended not for having a superior explanatory system, but for recognizing, in the words of the later Wittgenstein, that explanations come to an end somewhere: rather than serving as the basis of an ultimate "super account," the appeal to God or fate is, for the *Tractatus*, an acknowledgment that there is a point at which nothing more can be said.

Of course, it may now begin to sound as if Wittgenstein is claiming that there are in fact genuine questions that science or human reason can never answer, that his philosophical task is ultimately one of limiting reason's scope in this regard. But we note that in the passage above it is held that, in one respect, the moderns are *right* in treating natural laws as unassailable, as providing a complete answer. They are right because, as Wittgenstein has aimed to bring out throughout the

Tractatus, outside of the scope of the sciences our purported explanations of the world are merely pseudo-accounts. For him, it is thus not a matter of placing a prohibition on reason's ability to address certain kinds of questions, but rather of showing that those questions are not genuine questions in the first place;[11] once more the deepest problems are held to be no problems at all. Wittgenstein's praise of the ancients, however, connotes an attempt to caution against arriving too quickly at this insight, against supposing too readily that our fundamental questions have truly dissolved. The real thrust of this passage, we might then say, is to suggest that an easy satisfaction with the results of science is the wrong kind of satisfaction. We must not deceive ourselves about who we are, about what we ultimately believe. We must not mistake indifference or obtuseness for a genuine understanding of what Wittgenstein calls the "sense of life" (6.521). Instead, it is only when we face honestly our experience of our lives as problematic that we can hope to attain the sort of insight, the redemption that he envisions.

The *Tractatus* then seeks to get us to see how philosophical perplexities can be expressions – indeed the complete embodiment – of that fundamentally problematic relation to the world. Over and over, the text attempts to expose the different guises of philosophical disquietude: as the demand that the picture's fundamental relation to the world be once and for all secured, as the need for a theory of types to prevent nonsense, as the attempt to set down a formal specification of the laws of thought. And over and over we are to see in response how, in the words of 5.473, logic must take care of itself. We are to see, that is, how there is after all nothing for us to *do* to satisfy these kinds of concerns, how it is the concerns themselves that are the source of our fundamental unease. In gaining clarity about our philosophical confusions we can then be said to be liberated from the *problem* of life, the sense that our fundamental relationship to the world is something that requires a straightforward solution. Thus Wittgenstein intersperses remarks about the disappearance of philosophical problems with claims about the appropriate way of living in general: "The solution of the problem of life is seen in the vanishing of the problem. (Is not this the reason why those who have found after a long period of doubt that the sense of life became clear to them have then been unable to say what constituted that sense?)" (TLP 6.521).[12]

If, for the *Tractatus,* philosophy comes to stand for our fundamental estrangement from the world, it is then in the disappearance of philosophy that our redemption lies.[13]

We can now return to our question of how this text's own remarks are to be generalized to all of philosophy. The above considerations have been intended to bring out more sharply the basis for our fundamental contention throughout that this text's usage of the predicate "nonsense" cannot be assimilated to the ordinary usage of a predicate like "red." For while we can make straightforwardly meaningful judgments about the application of the latter, what we are now seeing more clearly is that the ascription of the string "nonsense" signals, for Wittgenstein, a basic shift in our orientation toward the world. My willingness to invoke this term carries with it the recognition not simply that some string of signs is illegitimate and must be withdrawn but, rather, that the impulse leading to the utterance of those signs is itself questionable.[14] It is, Wittgenstein might say, my very *will* that is at issue when I characterize philosophy – my own philosophical utterances – as nonsense.[15] But that is then to suggest that the possibility of "going on" with the Tractarian enterprise is misdescribed when it is as presented as the problem of determining the future applicability of the term "nonsense." Rather than aiming to bring me to use a word (or a whole set of words – "fact," "thing," "logic," and so on) in a new manner, Wittgenstein seeks to change my whole way of viewing, my fundamental attitude toward, philosophy: I am now to see the philosophical activity as *essentially* an attempt to make impossible demands on language and the world. This is not to deny that philosophical questions might arise for me after I have read – and understood – the *Tractatus.* But Wittgenstein assumes that once we have grasped the insight at the heart of this text such questions will no longer tempt us. I will now see persistence in the activity of philosophizing as an indication that my will is at odds with reality,[16] that I am refusing to accept fully the course of my experience.[17] It will be taken as a sign that something has gone awry in my way of living. And that is to say that to "go on" with the task of the *Tractatus* is ultimately just to acknowledge the "must" in the text's final remark – "Whereof one cannot speak, thereof one *must* remain silent" (TLP 7) – as the mark not of logical necessity but of ethical obligation.

III

Wittgenstein, of course, will seemingly violate his own ethical maxim, and quite egregiously: the rest of his life is spent speaking of those things of which we must remain silent. This principle might thus seem to be worse than empty, for besides not even binding its own author, it serves to attach the stain of sin to philosophical inquiry. Are we now to view philosophy as a shameful activity, my engagement in it a sign of my corrupt character? Does Wittgenstein's inability to resist its allure not mark him as one who lacks the courage of his own convictions? It is tempting here to strongly resist these conclusions, to close our study with an unequivocal endorsement of Wittgenstein's practice and of philosophy generally. For with regard to the former, it is undeniably the case that Wittgenstein's later engagement in philosophy is something other than a mere repetition of his Tractarian views; rather, as we have discussed, he is involved in deepening his original insight, and in so doing gives up the early governing idea of an essential confusion from which we can be essentially liberated. In the *Investigations'* vision of philosophy, "Problems are solved (difficulties eliminated), not a *single* problem" (PI 133; emphasis Wittgenstein's). There are, for the later figure, endless philosophical confusions, endlessly various in their form, and hence an endless process of philosophical clarification.[18] What Wittgenstein comes to see, then, is that the whole idea of philosophy as *a* "fundamental" impulse toward the world cannot be sustained.

Such a shift would appear to go some way toward revoking the *Tractatus'* requirement of a kind of absolute philosophical silence; perhaps Wittgenstein may then be deemed innocent of the more serious charge of hypocrisy. The acceptance of this general picture seems to clear a space for our own continued involvement in philosophy as well. For insofar as we too are forever being caught in the snare of philosophical perplexities, we too must continually attempt to wriggle free from their grip – silence in this circumstance would betoken no more than a refusal to acknowledge the reality of our own confusion. Philosophy for us thus becomes not a ladder, ascended once and then permanently cast aside, but a *path* of clarification. The *Tractatus* may then be reinterpreted as the means of starting us down this route and alerting us to many of its central features.

Still, we must temper the familiar impulse to suppose that, given these seemingly more modest aspirations, we are now (finally) in possession of an entirely reliable method of philosophizing – as if, with Wittgenstein, the nagging questions about the ultimate value of philosophical activity have once and for all been put to rest. After all, Wittgenstein's "method," early and late, depends always on the possibility of bringing us to confront the core of the "problems of philosophy," with all their attendant slipperiness, their capacity to mystify and captivate. And that is to say that his attempt to *free* us from metaphysical confusion can just as easily serve to lead us more resoundingly into its depths. Nor is this a mere idle possibility, as the deeply metaphysical history of Tractarian scholarship might suggest. What does this mean for our understanding of the fundamental point of the book, of the dialectical approach it exemplifies? How stable is the state of ultimate clarity with which this text tantalizes us? If the *Tractatus* wants us to understand philosophy as, at its heart, nothing but illusion, it also teaches that philosophical reflection is itself our means of escape. For Wittgenstein, it would seem, liberation comes only by way of the most uncertain of paths.

NOTES

Preface

1. See PI 97–133. An even more extended discussion of the issue is found in the "Big Typescript," sections 86–93 (PO 161–199).

Introduction

1. See also the occurrences of the phrase *erloesende Wort* at NB 39 and 54, and the use of the term *erloesende* and its cognates at PG 193, CV 33, and D 69, 75, 87, 99, 101.
2. I am here alluding to – and placing this book among – the cluster of "nonstandard" interpretations of the *Tractatus* that would include Cerbone (2000), Conant (1989, 1991, 1993, 1998, 2000), Diamond (1991a, 1991b), Dreben (unpublished), Floyd (1998, in press), Goldfarb (unpublished), Kremer (1997), Ricketts (1996), Winch (1992), Witherspoon (2000). Friedlander (1992) might be included here as well. The clash between these new readings of the *Tractatus* and the more traditional interpretations, most recently defended by Hacker (2000) and Pears (unpublished), forms the immediate backdrop of this study, and will be discussed in some detail in this Introduction. McGinn (1999) discusses this conflict and attempts to develop a kind of synthesis of the two approaches; Reid (1998) offers a criticism of the Conant/Diamond position in particular, but without completely embracing what she calls a "metaphysical" position. Biletzki (in press) also offers an overview of the debate, in the context of a much broader and more detailed survey of Tractarian interpretations.
3. This translation is from the original Ogden version of the *Tractatus*. I will generally rely on the Ogden version for quotations, but will occasionally take recourse to the Pears/McGuinness translation.
4. Ramsey (1931).
5. Black (1964)
6. Stenius (1960).

7. Hintikka and Hintikka (1986).
8. Hacker (1986).
9. Pears (1987).
10. Such attempts to disregard or downplay the significance of 6.54 need not be understood as mere oversights on the part of commentators. Instead, some justification for this strategy can be offered: one might, for example, suggest (as Pears did in a 1998 meeting of the Boston Colloquium for Philosophy of Science) that this remark was inserted by Wittgenstein at the close of the book simply as a means of protecting himself from criticism. Of course, it remains for such an interpretation to account for 4.1272 at the center of the *Tractatus,* whose implication would seem to be much the same as 6.54; also, it must explain the remarks in the *Notebooks* on pages 45 and 50, where Wittgenstein is already found to be asserting that claims about the existence of simple objects – the sort of seemingly meaningful claim that dominates the opening section of the *Tractatus* – are nonsensical. But my central point is that the invocation of such passages is unlikely to be conclusive; their significance too can be downplayed. And that is to say that there is no easy or straightforward way to settle this interpretive dispute.
11. See, for example, Carnap (1979) for a statement of this way of responding to Wittgenstein's text. We must of course bear in mind that Carnap is writing always as a philosopher himself, and not simply as an expositor of Wittgenstein. He in fact explicitly acknowledges that his own position may differ from that of the *Tractatus* (see pp. 37–8 of *Philosophy and Logical Syntax*).
12. In the language of the *Tractatus,* we could say that Carnap views such formal assertions as *sinnlos* rather than *unsinnig.* Still, the real force of characterizing logical proposition as tautologies is itself, like almost everything in the *Tractatus,* very delicate and open to a variety of interpretations. See Dreben and Floyd (1991) for an excellent discussion of the shifting senses of the notion of tautology.
13. Anscombe (1959).
14. Geach (1976).
15. Hintikka and Hintikka (1986).
16. Hacker espouses such a position in his classic work *Insight and Illusion* (1986). He presents a more forceful argument for this view, however, in his recent response (2000) to Cora Diamond's way of reading the *Tractatus.*
17. Diamond (1991). Warren Goldfarb (unpublished) independently argued for a related position in an unpublished but frequently noted 1979 paper. Dreben (unpublished), and Floyd (1998, in press) have also more or less independently articulated a similar interpretation of the text. As I mention in footnote 2, James Conant (1989, 1991, 1993, 1998, 2000) and a number of other commentators have further elaborated the Diamond view.
18. Ramsey (1931).
19. Diamond (1991, p. 185).

20. Diamond (1991, p. 197) introduces this expression as a way of describing "a is an object," the sort of sentence that Wittgenstein explicitly dismisses as a "nonsense pseudo-sentence" (TLP 4.1272). But clearly her contention is that his own seemingly positive assertions have exactly the same status.
21. "Jabberwocky" is put forth by Diamond (1991, p. 96) as an example of the kind of thing Wittgenstein has in mind whenever he speaks of philosophical nonsense.
22. Diamond (1991, pp. 95–114).
23. Conant (1991, pp. 341–2; 1998, pp. 244–50; 2000, pp. 194–5) tends to emphasize this point quite strongly as well, arguing that, for Wittgenstein, philosophical nonsense resists logical segmentation and thus cannot be understood as resulting from the illegitimate combination of intrinsically intelligible components. Aside from my concerns, discussed above, about leaning too heavily on this particular formulation, I also worry that it can lead to attributing to Wittgenstein just the sort of theoretical doctrine that Conant most wants to avoid – as if Wittgenstein's central aim were now understood as one of giving an elaborate *account* of the nature of nonsense. Instead, it seems that we should say that the distinction, implicit especially in 5.4733, between what Conant calls the "substantial" and "austere" conceptions of nonsense (2000, p. 176) belongs to the internal apparatus of the *Tractatus,* and as such should be seen as having the same status as the show/say distinction, the conception of logic as tautologous, and so forth.
24. Hacker (2000, p. 361) makes a similar point (although in a rather more contentious manner), suggesting that Diamond surreptitiously introduces a distinction between "plain nonsense" and "transitional nonsense."
25. See Diamond (2000).
26. Conant (1991, p. 344; 1993, p. 216; 2000, p. 198) also emphasizes this distinction.
27. Diamond (2000, pp. 157–8).
28. Diamond (2000, pp. 158–60).
29. Reid (1998, p. 130) makes a similar point.
30. Goldfarb (1997, pp. 70–2) argues in much the same way in his discussion of Diamond's *The Realistic Spirit.*
31. Indeed, Hacker (2000, p. 362) tries to use something very much like this claim as a *reductio* of the Conant/Diamond reading of the *Tractatus.*
32. Goldfarb (1997) again makes something like this point with his remark that, for Wittgenstein, " 'nonsense' cannot really be a general term of criticism" (p. 71). Floyd (in press, p. 44) makes a similar assertion. Diamond, in her response to Goldfarb (1997, p. 80), appears to acknowledge the problem, understanding it as the question of whether Wittgenstein has "a *general* approach to the issue of irresoluteness." She does not, however, attempt to provide a determinate answer.
33. Conant (1989, p. 266) presumably is saying something of this sort when he holds "I, over and over again, want to say something like this: 'Wittgenstein's (or Kierkegaard's) teaching cannot be stated, it can only be shown'."

34. In viewing this most dogmatic-seeming of texts as intrinsically dialectical, I am to some extent following Dreben (unpublished), Floyd (1998), Putnam (1998), and Goldfarb (unpublished, 1997). Needless to say, the idea of dialectic is rather slippery – I do not attempt to define this term – and I make no claim to be using it in exactly the same sense as any of these authors (indeed, it is not clear that they all understand "dialectical" in just the same way either). I think it is safe to say, however, if I may be forgiven the employment of a piece of Wittgenstein jargon, that there is at least a family resemblance amongst all these various uses of the notion.
35. See pp. 12–13.
36. Again this point is essentially made in the Preface, when Wittgenstein asserts: "In order to be able to draw a limit to thought, we should have to find both sides of the limit thinkable (i.e., we should have to be able to think what cannot be thought)" (TLP, p. 3).
37. The key passage from this letter reads: "The book's point is an ethical one. I once meant to include in the preface a sentence which is not in fact there now but which I will write out for you here, because it will perhaps be a key to the work for you. What I meant to write, then, was this: My work consists of two parts: the one presented here plus all I have *not* written. And it is precisely this second part that is the important one. My book draws limits to the sphere of the ethical from the inside as it were, and I am convinced that this is the ONLY *rigorous* way of drawing those limits" (LF 95).
38. See CV 32–3.
39. Conant (1991, pp. 352–4) makes a similar point.
40. Hacker (2000, pp. 371–82) emphasizes this point as part of his argument against the Conant/Diamond reading of the *Tractatus*.
41. See, for example, Wittgenstein's 1931 discussion of the Tractarian understanding of the forms of the elementary propositions. After remarking that he quite rightly held in the *Tractatus* that those forms could not be specified in advance, he goes on: "Yet I did think that the elementary propositions could be specified at a later date. Only in recent years have I broken away from that mistake. At the time I wrote in a manuscript of my book (this is not printed in the *Tractatus*), The answers to philosophical questions must never be surprising. In philosophy you cannot discover anything. I myself, however, had not clearly understood this and offended against it" (VC 183). Note here how a specific alteration in one of the claims of the *Tractatus*, and the seemingly theoretical description of the earlier position as a "mistake," go along with Wittgenstein's suggestion that he had not truly understood the anti-theoretical character of his own thinking. The mistake here, in other words, would not appear to consist in a false assertion in the ordinary sense but, rather, just in the implied assimilation of philosophical claims to those claims that *could* be false (or true); such an assimilation, Wittgenstein suggests, runs counter to the spirit of the *Tractatus*.

Chapter I

1. Nonetheless, many commentators have insisted on characterizing the *Tractatus* as an essentially realist work; see, e.g., Allaire (1966, pp. 325–41), Stenius (1960), Hacker (1981, pp. 85–107), Pears (1987, p. 26), Dummet (1991). Moreover, even when such a view has been challenged, it has often been by attempting to place the text into some *other* standard philosophical niche. Thus, for example, Williams (1974) argues that the *Tractatus* is in fact a (transcendental) idealist tract; while Copi (1966) and Anscombe (1959) see Wittgenstein as advocating a certain brand of nominalism. 5.64 alone seems to suggest the hollowness of this whole debate.
2. See Mounce (1981, p. 19).
3. Wittgenstein, in a discussion with Desmond Lee in 1930 or 1931, is in fact explicit about the dual role of the term "logic": "Logic may mean two things: (1) a logical calculus as e.g. the *Principia Mathematica* (2) the philosophy of logic" (CL 110).
4. Friedlander (1992, p. 83) also characterizes the role of the object in the *Tractatus* in something like this manner, referring to the object as a "condition for the possibility" of the fact.
5. Cf. also 2.0131: "A spatial object must lie in infinite space. (A point in space is an argument place). A speck in a visual field need not be red, but it must have a color; it has, so to speak, a color space round it. A tone must have *a* pitch, the object of the sense of touch *a* hardness, etc." Once more, Wittgenstein makes it clear that the object is to be identified with the thing in its space of possibilities: it is this red speck taken together with its capacity to be blue, green, yellow, etc.; this tone taken together with all the other pitches it could assume; and so forth.
6. See "Function and Concept" (CP 141).
7. A good deal of the literature on the *Tractatus* in fact involves debates over which one of these sorts of notions Wittgenstein "really" means when he speaks of an object.
8. In light of this point, the standard attempt to accommodate Tractarian objects within traditional philosophical categories seems particularly misguided. For it is not simply that Wittgenstein suggests that, as it turns out, we cannot settle *a priori* whether objects are sense data, particulars, universals, or what have you. Instead, part of his purpose in introducing the notion in the way that he does is precisely to *lead us away from* this kind of logical categorizing. To attempt to explain the real nature of objects is to be engaged in an endeavor that is not only fruitless, but also fundamentally obscures Wittgenstein's real purpose.
9. See, for example, Weinberg (1966, pp. 75–85); Pears (1987, pp. 27–8, 66–72); and Fogelin (1996, pp. 14–17).
10. This will be discussed in Chapter II of this study.
11. At this point, the *Tractatus* is clearly anticipating 3.221: "Objects I can only

name. Signs represent them. I can only speak *of* them. I cannot *assert them.* A proposition can only say how a thing is, not what it is."

12. Cf. NB 52: "The name of a complex functions in the proposition like the name of an object that I only know by *description.* – The proposition that depicts it functions as a description." Cf. also this remark from two days earlier: " 'Complex sign' and 'proposition' are *equivalent*" (NB 52).
13. Friedlander (1992) makes a similar point; see pp. 84–5.
14. This is the position taken by Black (1964, pp. 58–62), as well as by Mounce (1981, pp. 19–21). I suggest that thus framing the issue in terms of a need for "immediate contact" between language and the world stems from viewing Wittgenstein as ultimately resting on a Russellian notion of "knowledge by acquaintance." But we have seen that a quite different conception of simplicity would seem to be operating in the *Tractatus.*
15. Cf. TLP 5.473, which directly mirrors language from the opening remark of the *Notebooks:* "Logic must take care of itself. A *possible* sign must also be able to signify."
16. Recall from the Introduction (pp. 14–15) our contention that the whole *Tractatus* can be conceived as an attempt to characterize precisely *the* philosophical question.
17. See, for example, Black's introduction to the *Tractatus'* discussion of the picture: "Having concluded this account of the world as a mosaic of atomic facts embedded in logical space, Wittgenstein now turns to consider what is necessarily involved in any symbolic *representation* of the world. The leading question might be expressed as: Given that this is what the world must be, what *must* language be, in order to be capable of representing the world adequately? The task may be called, in Wittgenstein's own phraseology, that of clarifying the essence of all language, provided 'language' is taken to include any system of signs, not necessarily verbal, that is adequate for making all possible assertions about reality" (1964, p. 72).
18. Schwyzer (1966, pp. 277–8), Stripling (1978, pp. 32, 75–81), and Friedlander (1992, p. 96) also focus on this aspect of the picture theory.
19. Here I follow Friedlander (1992) in translating *vorstellen,* a term that Ogden here renders as "represent," always as "present." This is done to mark a systematic distinction from Wittgenstein's use of the term *darstellen,* which, again like Friedlander, I translate as "represent." The role of *darstellen* will be discussed in Chapter III.
20. Note that also mentioned here in connection with the negative fact is the term *Sachlage* (translated by Ogden as "state of affairs"). The significance of this third way of speaking a fact will not be discussed until Chapter III. For the time being, it is sufficient to bear in mind that a single *Sachlage* appears to comprise both an existent and a nonexistent *Sachverhalt.*
21. See, for example, Mounce (1981, pp. 23–5).
22. Black (1964, pp. 77–8).
23. See, for example, *Principles of Mathematics,* p. 427.

24. Recall that I always use this word as a translation of Wittgenstein's *vorstellen*.
25. The *Tractatus* is in this way sometimes assumed to rest on the postulation of a fundamental "isomorphism" between language and the world. Hacker (1986, p. 61) and Stenius (1960, pp. 91–6), among others, put forward this idea. Black (1964, pp. 69, 90–1) prefers the term "homomorphism" but holds to the same basic notion of the centrality of this "hypothesis" to the *Tractatus'* view.
26. This difficulty in assessing Wittgenstein's real orientation toward the question at hand calls to mind his remark in *Zettel* 314: "Here we come up against a remarkable and characteristic phenomenon in philosophical investigation: the difficulty – I might say – is not that of finding the solution but rather that of recognizing as the solution something that looks as if it were only a preliminary to it. 'We have already said everything. – Not anything that follows from this, no, *this* itself is the solution!' This is connected, I believe, with our wrongly expecting an explanation, whereas the solution of the difficulty is a description, if we give it the right place in our considerations. If we dwell upon it and do not try to get beyond it. The difficulty here is: to stop."
27. Cf. NB 108.
28. This point will be key in understanding how Wittgenstein views the sense of a proposition. For, as we shall see, it is a central tenet of the *Tractatus* that the proposition's sense – the thought that it expresses – is not given by any external features of the propositional sign. Cf. TLP 4.002: "Language disguises the thought; so that from the external form of the clothes one cannot infer the form of the thought they clothe, because the external form of the clothes is constructed with quite another object than to let the form of the body be recognized." Cf. also this remark from "Notes on Logic": "Distrust of grammar is the first requisite for philosophizing" (NL 106).
29. The same point could be made using the idea of music, the metaphor that we find at 4.011–4.0141. The fact that we can, for example, clap along with a song is in one sense arbitrary: there is no necessity that we correlate hand claps rather than, say, the clicks of a finger with the "2" and the "4" of each measure. But that we can represent the time in *some* such way is not arbitrary – it is integral to this piece of music being the kind of thing that it is (as is evident if we think of the ludicrousness of the attempt to clap along with a novel). Wittgenstein would then say that the possibility of representing the rhythm of this song by means of hand claps ultimately depends on a commonality of form.
30. He also seems to suggest this idea in NB 37.
31. By contrast, the mathematical notion of an isomorphism conceives of a 1–1 function mapping one *independently* given domain onto another.
32. Here one begins to feel the real force of the earlier point about the "simplicity" of objects, about how their forms only emerge through the structure of the atomic fact.

33. We may leave it an open question as to whether the *Tractatus* will ultimately count space as one of the *logical* forms – that is, as one of the fundamental categories of thought or language that will be made manifest in the elementary propositions. It is thus not yet decided whether "space" is put forward as an *example* of the results of logical analysis or as a mere analogy. The issue of the relation between the notions of pictorial and logical form and their relation to Wittgenstein's conception of analysis will be addressed in the next chapter.
34. See pp. 12–13.
35. See also Introduction to the current study for a more general discussion of this issue, especially of Cora Diamond's way of criticizing the standard reading.
36. Pears (1987, p. 143).
37. Here one is of course reminded of Russell's response to the show/say distinction in the Introduction to the *Tractatus.* Russell (p. 23) famously suggests that, while it may be impossible to express the underlying structure of a language in that same language, nothing would seem to preclude the possibility of another language serving this function; such a hierarchy of languages, he holds, might indeed be infinite.
38. Pears (1987, p. 143).
39. Pears (1987, p. 144).
40. Note that the term *abbilden* is thus distinguished from *vorstellen* (and, as we shall see, from *darstellen* as well). Whereas a picture "presents" the existence and nonexistence of a certain set of atomic facts (and "represents" a possibility of such facts), it only "depicts" reality or the world. The distinction, then, is between a picture's relation to some specific set of facts and its fundamental role *as* a picture: just by virtue of being what it is, a picture (*Bild*) depicts (*abbildet*) reality.

Chapter II

1. Pears (1987, p. 136) also raises this issue.
2. See pp. 102–07 of Friedlander (1992) for his discussion of this issue. Friedlander suggests a distinction between the pictorial form, as the condition of the possibility of the picture as a *fact,* and the logical form, as the condition of the picture-fact's capacity to *represent* some particular state of affairs. According to Friedlander, then, the logical form has to do with how we use the picture as a whole to state something about the world; this notion is thus quite connected with the account of the so-called logical constants. Now, as will become increasingly evident, I take as extremely important this distinction between the inner composition of the picture and its use in representing particular states of affairs. But I do not believe that the notion of logical form is to be connected with the latter. For, if nothing else, this assimilation would appear to fly in the face of 2.181 ("If the pictorial form is the logical form, then the picture is called a logical picture."): it does not seem to make sense to speak, even

hypothetically, of a situation in which the pictorial form *is* the logical form if these notions correspond to the very different dimensions of the picture that Friedlander describes.

3. Here I am to some extent echoing the position of Black (1964, pp. 88–91), who distinguishes the "homologous" relation holding between the arrangement of picture elements and reality in a logical picture from the "identity" that characterizes the corresponding relation in, e.g., a spatial picture. Unlike Black, however, I am reading Wittgenstein as ultimately concerned to show that, whether we speak of a logical picture *or* a spatial one, the "relation" between picture elements and their real world counterparts is not a genuine one. Cf. also Fogelin (1976, pp. 19–20) on this issue.
4. See Stern (1995, pp. 39–43) for a good account of Wittgenstein's later rejection of the picture theory, of how the notion of a picture shifts from a way of characterizing (in *some* sense) the proposition to a way of describing the basis of the drive toward philosophical theorizing.
5. See, for example, Sellars (1966, pp. 249–51), Evans (1966, pp. 133–5), Anscombe (1959, pp. 98–101), Copi (1966, pp. 177–8), and, more recently, Ricketts (1996), for all of whom this remark provides evidence that properties and relations are not Tractarian objects.
6. This was Ramsey's (1931) view of the *Tractatus'* position. From what we have already seen about Wittgenstein's conception of objects, such an interpretation cannot, in general, be altogether incorrect. But in its insistence on relying on understanding the basic constituents of the atomic fact in terms of traditional philosophical categories, it misses what we have suggested to be Wittgenstein's real point about our relation to those forms – how it is nonsense to suppose that they could be given *a priori.* Moreover, as I argue immediately below, none of these issues is directly relevant to the real concern of 3.1432.
7. Or, we could say, it is a contingent or nonessential feature of the particular pictorial method of representation used in our example that in it no proxies for spatial relations will appear.
8. In this respect, Wittgenstein's discussion is in fact linked to Russell's early worries over accounting for the peculiar unity that seems to distinguish a proposition from a mere list of its constituents (see, e.g., *Principles of Mathematics*, pp. 38, 51–2, 83–4).
9. The notion that, in addition to acquaintance with objects, acquaintance with a logical *form* is a prerequisite for the possibility of judgment is discussed by Russell in *Theory of Knowledge* (see, e.g., pp. 99, 111), as well as in *The Philosophy of Logical Atomism.* By this time, Russell no longer countenances propositions as genuine entities and thus is not concerned to account for *their* unity, but the problem of the unity of the judgment has a similar structure.
10. Frege uses this language in "Function and Concept" and "Concept and Object." Now, of course, one might say that Frege's resorting to metaphor here is an indication that, like Wittgenstein, he recognizes the impossibility

of giving any sort of genuine account of the proposition's unity. This, I take it, would be part of the force of Ricketts' insistence on the primacy of the judgment in Frege's thought (see, e.g., Ricketts [1986]). Even so, Frege does seem to speak as if there might ultimately be a fact of the matter with regard to the question of the nature of the relation of function and object, only such a fact is unavailable to us; certainly such a perception is given by Frege's remark that the distinction between functions and objects is "founded on the nature of our language" (CP 194). It is essential then to see how contrary such a position is to the Wittgensteinian view, as I am presenting it.

11. And here, of course, we are called back not only to 2.15, but also to 2.03: "In the atomic fact objects hang one in another, like the links of a chain."
12. One might suppose that this remark would have served to steer commentators away from vain speculation about possible examples of Tractarian elementary propositions, but this has not always been the case. See, for example, Hintikka and Hintikka's (1986) attempt to construe such propositions as statements about "immediate experience" (pp. 74–80).
13. See pp. 41 ff.
14. See also TLP 5.563: "All propositions of our colloquial language are actually, just as they are, logically completely in order."
15. Here this key passage from *Philosophical Grammar* is especially pertinent: "Formerly, I myself spoke of a 'complete analysis', and I used to believe that philosophy had to give a definitive dissection of propositions so as to set out clearly all their connections and remove all possibilities of misunderstanding. I spoke as if there was a calculus in which such a dissection would be possible. I vaguely had in mind something like the definition that Russell had given for the definite article, and I used to think that in a similar way one would be able to use visual impressions etc. to define the concept say of a sphere, and thus exhibit once for all the connections between the concepts and lay bare the source of all misunderstandings, etc." (PG 211).
16. Note that in "Some Remarks on Logical Form," it is just this sort of procedure that Wittgenstein describes when he offers an example of the partial analysis of the sentence "Color patch P is red." Thus, he imagines setting up a coordinate system that would enable us to represent the shape and position of every patch of color in our visual system. While he offers no sample analysis of "red" itself, he makes clear that it would be treated in the same manner – that is, by setting up a mode of representation that allows for the full range of possible color ascriptions.
17. In this conception of analysis, I suggest we can see how the *Tractatus* might be said to assimilate generality to logical sum or product, just as Wittgenstein in *Philosophical Grammar* claims that it did (see PG 268 ff.). This later criticism has long puzzled commentators, since the *Tractatus* at 5.521 apparently rebukes *Frege* and *Russell* for confusing generality with logical sum/product. How then, Tractarian readers have wondered, can Wittgenstein have been involved in the same confusion himself? The

above discussion brings out how, in supposing that the sense of a quantified statement could be captured through a specification of its instances, Wittgenstein is *implicitly* committed to viewing the quantifier as somehow derived from disjunction or conjunction. This in fact is precisely how he describes his mistake in *Philosophical Grammar:* "The [explanation of (∃ϕx as a logical sum and of (x).ϕx as a logical product] went with an incorrect notion of logical analysis in that I thought that some day the logical product for a particular (x).ϕx would be found" (PG 268). My suggestion, then, is that while the early Wittgenstein attempts to distinguish the grammar of generality from that of the truth functions, he comes to see later that he had not done this with sufficient sharpness.

18. Cf. Hylton's (1997) claim: "Such a conception of sense is possible because Wittgenstein does not accept that our thoughts are, so to speak, transparent to us. He does not accept, that is to say, that if I have one thought I must know what thought it is, that if I have two thoughts I must know whether they are the same, and so on" (p. 92).
19. The attraction of solipsism for Wittgenstein – part of the reason why he will say at 5.62 that what solipsism means is quite correct – is already evident in these passages. Just as he will then deflate the "truth" of solipsism by equating it with pure realism (see TLP 5.64), however, we must come to see here the insubstantiality of the claim that logical analysis deals only with "my" sense. The way in which such a claim might be said to be misleading should become apparent as we go along.
20. Nonetheless, many commentators, beginning with Russell in the Introduction, have in fact assumed Wittgenstein's talk of "determinateness" to suggest that he is working within something like a Fregean framework. Thus Russell writes: "[Wittgenstein] is concerned with the conditions for accurate Symbolism, i.e., for Symbolism in which a sentence 'means' something quite definite. In practice, language is always more or less vague, so that what we assert is never quite precise" (p. 8). See also Pears (1987, p. 73, n. 40).
21. See, for example, p. 68 of *The Foundations of Arithmetic,* where Frege asserts that a proper definition of number must be able to tell us whether or not Julius Caesar is a number.
22. This is stated more or less explicitly by Frege in "Function and Concept" (CP 148) and "On Sense and Reference" (CP 169), among other places.
23. Black (1964, p. 112) makes a similar point.
24. Ironically, we might say that something like the same insight lies behind Frege's way of demanding determinateness of sense; for in requiring that concepts be defined for all arguments he too is acknowledging that the meaningful assertion in some sense cannot leave any possibilities open. But Frege unwittingly undermines his own insight (at least from Wittgenstein's point of view) by supposing that such determinacy must be somehow secured by us prior to the application of my concepts to the world. This presupposes that circumstances might arise that would lead us to shift our assessment about the meaningfulness of our assertions: for

Frege, if my judgment contains a concept "ϕ" which, it turns out, fails to be defined for some argument "a" (an argument that I may not have anticipated when introducing the concept), I will conclude that this judgment, and all those containing "ϕ" lack a Bedeutung. But this seems to imply that it is up to the *world* ultimately to determine whether or not my judgment makes sense. Frege in this way imagines a kind of divorce between language and its users – as if we could draw a general distinction between what *I* think I mean by my utterance and what I *in fact* mean. For Wittgenstein, though, this is nothing but an admission of the intrinsic *in*determinacy of sense and hence a fundamental misconstrual of the role of logic.

25. This conception of the name is, of course, familiar from Russell's famous distinction between knowledge by acquaintance and knowledge by description.
26. This is a conclusion reminiscent of Pears's (1987) reading of the picture theory. See especially pp. 142–4.
27. See Ricketts (1986, pp. 65–96).
28. See VC 46.
29. Here I suggest that we can see the origin of Wittgenstein's interest in the "seeing-as" phenomenon discussed especially in Part II of *Philosophical Investigations.*
30. See pp. 55–6.
31. Cf. this remark from the first appendix to "Notes on Logic": "It is to be remembered that names are not things, but classes: "A" is the same letter as "A." This has the most important consequences for every symbolic language" (NB 102).
32. *Principles* xv.
33. Black (1964), for example, appears to understand Wittgenstein's criticisms in this manner, suggesting that "Wittgenstein's own programme for 'logical syntax' can properly be viewed as an attempt to accomplish what Russell was reaching for in his theory of types" (p. 146).
34. It is indeed just this interpretation that Carnap builds on in his *The Logical Syntax of Language.*
35. Moreover, as Dreben (unpublished) has pointed out, a little reflection will reveal that a syntactical approach in Hilbert's sense *couldn't* satisfy the aim of Tractarian logical syntax, assuming that, as 3.324 and 3.325 suggest, that aim is to rule out what Wittgenstein terms "nonsense." For how would such a standard meta-mathematical approach, a specification of a formal language in terms of a set of formation rules and a set of transformation rules, preclude expressions like "The world is everything that is the case" or "2 + 2 is at 3 o'clock equal to 4"? It is true that the mathematical logician will typically have no reason to include a name for "the world" or a predicate denoting "is at 3 o'clock" in his language, but that is not to say that this language "rules out" expressions formed from such notions (and, besides, if the avoidance of nonsense were simply a matter of refraining from the use of certain terms, this

could be accomplished in ordinary language as easily as in a formal language).

36. Black's technical interpretation of the criticism, by contrast, can only be maintained by ignoring the context of 3.331–3.333, as is evident from his characterization of these passages as "a digression," albeit "a highly interesting one" (1964, p. 145).
37. Cf. Hintikka and Hintikka (1986) and their claim about Wittgenstein's commitment to the "ineffability of semantics."
38. This is, of course, not to suggest that Tractarian differences of *Bedeutung* will correspond precisely to Russellian type theoretic distinctions. Russell, for example, would regard "x is brown" and "x is heavy" as belonging to the same type of propositional function, whereas, as we have seen, Wittgenstein would distinguish them (since "the surface of the table," e.g., can only meaningfully be substituted in the first). The point, though, as is illustrated in this example, is that Wittgenstein's approach is more fine-grained and will thus acknowledge *at least* those distinctions drawn by the theory of types.
39. It is presumably this sort of idea that leads Wittgenstein in *Philosophical Remarks* to declare that grammar – the descendant of Tractarian logical syntax – "is a 'theory of logical types' " (PR 7). The point here is not that the grammatical investigations characteristic of his later thought involve instituting *a priori* restrictions on sense of the kind that we find in the theory of types. Instead, Wittgenstein is saying that by describing clearly the role of certain problematic expressions, "grammar" is really seeking the same *end* sought by Russell – the avoidance of a certain sort of nonsense.
40. This example is used only for the sake of illustration, since Wittgenstein comes to see that color cannot ultimately constitute one of the logical forms. This recognition leads to the so-called color exclusion problem that is discussed in "Some Remarks on Logical Form."
41. See, for example, NB 20: "The internal relation between the proposition and its reference, the method of symbolizing – is the system of co-ordinates which projects the situation into the proposition. The proposition corresponds to the fundamental co-ordinates." In the persistent metaphor of the coordinate system, we no doubt see the influence of Wittgenstein's training as an engineer, but also, more specifically, the importance for him of Hertz. See Grasshof (1997) for a discussion of the influence of Hertz, although one that draws a very different picture of the nature of the *Tractatus*.
42. See Introduction to the present study.
43. This would seem to be the position of Cora Diamond, who holds that, for Wittgenstein, "the *whole* philosophical vocabulary reflected confusion" and hence that "we are all Benno Kerry's through and through" (1991, p. 184).
44. Admittedly, it is not entirely clear that such objections are in the end effectual against Frege either. After all, Frege in "Concept and Object"

acknowledges that he is using the term "concept" in a special sense, that is, to refer to something that is intrinsically predicative in nature. The *Begriffsschrift* could then in fact be seen as helpful in clarifying what that means, since it represents an example of a language in which certain kinds of signs are always used in this way. Such an interpretation of Frege's thought brings him closer to Wittgenstein, as Cora Diamond would have it, since the focus here is only on characterizing a particular expression. On the other hand, though, Frege does seem to want to claim more than just the right to employ a term in his own peculiar sense. For even in "Concept and Object" he speaks of his use of the term "concept" as "purely logical" (CP 182), suggesting that it is meant to reflect the necessary structure of our language. In this case, Frege does invite questions about the status of his Begriffsschrift, of logic generally – just the kind of question that I claim the *Tractatus* is most concerned to get us to ask.

45. Again we are called back to the opening of the Preface and the prerequisite for understanding the book's point that we have the same or similar thoughts as its author.
46. The notion of mathematical multiplicity also can help us make clearer Wittgenstein's claim about the uniqueness of analysis, a claim that is in fact reiterated at 3.3442: "The sign of the complex is not arbitrarily resolved in the analysis, in such a way that its resolution would be different in every propositional structure." To hold that there is a unique analysis of the proposition "The watch is on the table" is not to say that all acceptable analyses will literally make use of coordinate systems; such a choice is obviously arbitrary. Instead, the claim amounts to the assertion that, whatever the specific manner of expression chosen, in every analysis that is to count as complete the possibilities of combination of the simple signs – the sign system's "mathematical multiplicity" – will be the same.
47. We might, in fact, describe Wittgenstein's later recognition of the color exclusion problem in just these terms: as a result of reflection on what makes sense to say in ascriptions of color, Wittgenstein comes to see that his so-called ab-functions – the truth tables – do not have the right multiplicity (at least for the task he envisioned for them) and therefore must be either modified or rejected.
48. Such formulations, while perhaps helping to make clear why Wittgenstein suggests that the attempt to give an *a priori* specification of logical form is incoherent, appear to leave open the possibility of an *a posteriori* completion of the task. Indeed, is this not what the *Tractatus'* own program of analysis amounts to? This is a difficult, but quite central question to answer if we are to understand the development of Wittgenstein's thought. In brief, I would suggest that, in the *Tractatus,* he seems to suppose that the actual carrying out of an analysis into elementary propositions is no part of the task of logic (presumably just because it has an apparent *a posteriori* character) and that its completion would therefore be of no logico-philosophical interest (see, e.g., 5.5571). But early on in his

"middle period" he comes to regard his Tractarian reliance on the *possibility* of such an enterprise as illicit, as he makes clear in this remark to Waismann: "There is another mistake, which is much more dangerous and also pervades my whole book, and that is the conception that there are questions the answers to which will be found at a later date. It is held that, although a result is not known, there is a way of finding it. Thus I used to believe, for example, that it is the task of logical analysis to discover the elementary propositions. I wrote, We are unable to specify the form of elementary propositions, and that was quite correct too. It was clear to me that here at any rate there are no hypotheses and that regarding these questions we cannot proceed by assuming from the very beginning, as Carnap does, that the elementary propositions consist of two-place relations, etc. Yet I did think that the elementary propositions could be specified at a later date. Only in recent years have I broken from that mistake" (VC 182). I suggest that "breaking from that mistake" comes to involve actually engaging in the analysis that is only spoken of from afar in the *Tractatus*. That is, the grammatical inquiries that we find in the *Investigations* are really attempts to carry out (albeit in a revised form) the purely descriptive enterprise envisaged for Tractarian logical syntax. This is not to suggest that philosophy becomes for the later Wittgenstein an *a posteriori* discipline, but rather that he comes to see that the supposed sharp distinction between the *a priori* and the *a posteriori* must itself be given up.

49. Cf. also 5.557: "The *application* of logic decides what elementary propositions there are. What lies in its application logic cannot anticipate."
50. With this understanding of the ambiguity inherent in the notion of an object we also can make sense of the parenthetical remark at 4.123: "Here to the shifting use of the words 'property' and 'relation' there corresponds the shifting use of the word 'object'." Wittgenstein above had been commenting on the "internal relation" of brighter and darker that obtains between two different shades of blue; he then had remarked how it is "unthinkable that *these* two objects should not stand in this relation" (TLP 4.23). It now should be evident that "object" in this context would be said by him to designate a *form*, a possibility of a color, and thus, along with "property" and "relation" to have shifted its ordinary usage.
51. Implied here is the complete coextensiveness of "thinkability" and "logical possibility." It is not, in other words, that the notion of what we can think serves as a *criterion* of what is logically possible, but rather that these two notions are themselves internally related. We shall discuss this point in greater detail on pp. 90–4.
52. This point will be very important both in the *Tractatus'* account of tautology and in its characterization of the general form of the proposition.
53. Despite Wittgenstein's forcefulness in this remark, some commentators refuse to believe that he really intends to dismiss as incoherent the ideas at the center of the philosophy of logic. Thus, for example, Black (1964) insists that the term "pseudo-concept," which Wittgenstein uses in

connection with "object," "fact," etc., "should not be read pejoratively" (p. 202), as it only serves to mark a contrast with "proper concept." Now, it is not at once clear just why it wouldn't be pejorative to call a concept "improper." But presumably Black supposes that, in the manner of Carnap (whom he quotes in this context), we can use this new distinction between proper and pseudo-concepts to go on and do legitimate philosophical work; "pseudo-concept" constitutes, in effect, no more than a technical term. This, however, would be anathema to Wittgenstein. Indeed, I would suggest that the full recognition of how one's fundamental point can be shifted in this way – how one's attacks on the philosophical tradition can be neatly turned to form a new move *within* that tradition – motivates in large part the style of Wittgenstein's later writing. For his later insistence on staying at the level of the particular case reflects precisely the insight that one can *always* (or almost always) make sense out of a form of words, give it a new use, and hence that the *Tractatus'* attempt to perform a kind of wholesale eradication of philosophical nonsense was illegitimate.

54. We are here called back to the Introduction to this study and the discussion of the difficulties inherent in the endeavor to characterize the central point of the *Tractatus.*
55. See pp. 14–15.

Chapter III

1. The heart of the later Wittgensteinian rejection of the *Tractatus* is, we might say, just the recognition of such structure as illicit. For he comes to see the notion that all the Tractarian apparatus is somehow "given" along with a certain view of logic as a remnant of the "*a priori*-ism" that he is, throughout his life, most concerned to undermine – it is at odds, then, not only with his later beliefs, but also with the very perspective that the early text was seeking to present. Thus the later fascination with following a rule and how one step cannot be regarded as *determining* the next: this is just a way of tearing away the remaining shreds of any sense of an underlying *a priori* structure.
2. See pp. 37 ff.
3. Again I attribute this way of drawing the distinction between the Tractarian terms *vorstellen* and *darstellen* to Friedlander (1992, pp. 103–07), even if his interpretation of these notions is ultimately somewhat different from my own. I am following him in rendering the former always as "present" and the latter "represent." Few commentators have focused on Wittgenstein's use of these terms. Stenius (1960, pp. 98–9) notes the distinction, translating Wittgenstein's German by different English terms (*vorstellen* is rendered by him as "depict," *darstellen* as "present"). Nonetheless, he appears to assume that these words function more or less as synonyms in the *Tractatus;* for him, the crucial distinc-

tion is between *vorstellen* and *abbilden.* Black (1964, p. 76) explicitly asserts that *vorstellen* is used by Wittgenstein "interchangeably" with *darstellen.*

4. Note that Wittgenstein does use the same term here as in the *Tractatus* to describe this aspect of the picture's relation to reality. I am not suggesting, however, that his Tractarian usage of the words *darstellen* and *vorstellen* is at this point firmly established.
5. See pp. 57–8 of this study.
6. By "logical constant" I, of course, here mean "and," "or," "not," and "if-then." Much of what Wittgenstein says about these also holds for the quantifier, but, as 5.521 makes clear, this notion is sufficiently distinct as to require separate treatment.
7. See Anscombe (1959, pp. 105–6 fn) for a discussion of this issue.
8. It is interesting to compare the above *Notebooks* passage to the passage in the *Investigations,* which also deals with this notion: "Imagine a picture representing a boxer in a particular stance. Now this picture can be used to tell someone how he should stand, should hold himself; or how he should not hold himself; or how a particular man did stand in such-and-such a place; and so on. One might (using the language of chemistry) call this picture a proposition-radical. This will be how Frege thought of the 'assumption' " (PI p. 10). Just as in 1914, Wittgenstein would appear to understand this Fregean notion in accordance with his own idea of the presenting dimension of the picture.
9. This declaration in fact also appears at the very start of the *Notebooks.* See NB 2.
10. Cf. also 4.031: "In the proposition a state of affairs is, as it were, put together for the sake of experiment."
11. There is then an important difference here from the situation as regards the elementary propositions. For, as we have seen, the notion of an *a priori* analysis of the elementary propositions is held to be nonsensical. ("There cannot be a hierarchy of the forms of the elementary propositions. Only that which we ourselves construct can we foresee" (TLP 5.556).) Central to understanding Wittgenstein's point in presenting the general form of the proposition will then be to see how he abstracts away from the question of the inner constitution of the propositions he attempts to describe.
12. Something like this view finds expression in Pitcher (1964) and Hallet (1977), but is maintained most explicitly and extensively in Hacker (1972). See Goldfarb (unpublished) for an extremely clear and insightful criticism of these authors' positions on this issue.
13. Again, Hacker (1986) explicitly puts forward this interpretation: "The harmony between thought and reality seemed [to Wittgenstein in the *Tractatus*] forged by psychic structures ('the language of thought' as some cognitive psychologists today would have it). But this, it became evident [to the later Wittgenstein], was confused on many counts. As we have seen, expectation and its fulfillment, belief and what makes it true, desire

and its satisfaction *make contact in grammar.* These internal relations are not bound together by a shadowy mental intermediary" (p. 119).

14. Such a claim is found in many passages in Frege's writing. One nice summary of his standard view is found in "Logic": "Unlike ideas, thoughts do not belong to the individual mind (they are not subjective), but are independent of our thinking, and confront each one of us in the same way (objectively). They are not the product of thinking, but are only grasped by thinking. In this regard they are like physical bodies. What distinguishes them from physical bodies is that they are non-spatial and we could perhaps really go as far as to say that they are essentially timeless – at least inasmuch as they are immune from anything that could effect a change in their intrinsic nature. They are like ideas in being non-spatial" (PW 148).
15. Cf. also Frege's denials of the possibility of illogical thought at BLA 12–13 and FA 20–1.
16. Hacker (1986, p. 119).
17. Cf. also the end of 5.2341: "Denial reverses the sense of a proposition." This likewise makes it appear that the sense of a proposition is what is represented when that proposition is true.
18. See Chapter I, n. 20.
19. McDonough (1986, pp. 26–42) introduces the term "sense1" to, in effect, describe these "twin aspects" taken together; this is distinguished from the "sense2" of a proposition, which is a specification of whether the existence of that which corresponds to the sense$_1$ is to be "included" or "excluded" by the proposition. This is an interesting way of putting it, especially since McDonough's sense1 would seem to correspond to what Wittgenstein, early on, in the "Notes Dictated to G. E. Moore in Norway" refers to as the "Bedeutung" of the proposition. (See NB 112: "The *Bedeutung* of a proposition is the fact that corresponds to it, e.g., if our proposition be "aRb," if it's true, the corresponding fact would be the fact aRb, if false, the fact ~ aRb.") Nonetheless, McDonough's formulation is potentially misleading, since by dividing up the notion of sense in this way, it encourages the very sort of (Russellian) reification of facts that I claim Wittgenstein is attempting to undermine. I suggest that it is to avoid such a reification that Wittgenstein soon gives up talk of a proposition's Bedeutung, and in the *Tractatus* expresses what he was previously reaching for now with the notion of a picture "presenting" states of affairs. Emphasis on the *use* of the propositional/pictorial sign, one might say, comes largely to replace any early tendency toward the postulation of entities.
20. See Russell's claims in *Philosophy of Logical Atomism,* pp. 35–47, 70–78.
21. Such a view is attributed to Wittgenstein by Bradley (1992, p. 9), who explicitly equates Wittgenstein's position in the *Tractatus* with Russell's in *The Philosophy of Logical Atomism.*
22. This is what Wittgenstein means at 2.22 when he says that a picture represents what it represents "*through* the pictorial form."
23. See, for example, Black (1964, p. 90), Bradley (1992, pp. 151–2).

24. That, of course, simply means that the propositional constituent is here being used in a manner that is not consonant with its ordinary logico-syntactical employment. Thus Wittgenstein says that the sentence "Socrates is identical" makes no sense not because we have produced an illogical thought – we *cannot* go wrong at the level of the expression since, as we have seen, the expression is nothing but the sign in its significant use – but because "we have given *no* meaning to the word 'identical' as *adjective*" (TLP 5.4733). It is open to us to map the use of "identical" to that of, say, "wise," in this context and hence give the word a meaning, but without some such measure, we must recognize we have not as yet constructed a genuine proposition. See Diamond (1991, pp. 95–114) and Conant (1991, pp. 341–2; 1998, pp. 244–50; 2000, pp. 194–5) for an elaboration of this idea.
25. See pp. 6–7.
26. Juliet Floyd (1998) puts the general point well. Noting that what the *Tractatus* identifies as the *unsinnig* pseudo-propositions of philosophy, as well as the *sinnlos* tautologies and contradictions, nearly always take the form of sentences "which *obey* ordinary rules of grammar" she remarks: "Wittgenstein is questioning the idea that ordinary grammar is adequate to guarantee sense" (p. 84).
27. Fogelin (1996, pp. 46–7), seeing a tension in Wittgenstein's views, maintains that he does not in fact ultimately deny the status of propositionhood to the strings of logic. That is, his "theory of truth-functionality" forces him to grant that tautologies and contradictions are, in the end, legitimate combinations of signs, even if this acceptance comes with "grumbles from the side of the picture theory" expressed as 4.466's reference to these as "the disintegration of the combination of signs."
28. Fogelin (1996, p. 82) and Black (1964, pp. 318–19), among others, assume such an interpretation of the *Tractatus*. Thus, Black maintains: "The need for known decision procedures for checking on putative logical truths is an integral and indispensable feature of Wittgenstein's philosophy of logic. For he would find it intolerable that we might understand a proposition without knowing in advance how to find out whether it was a tautology or contradiction; he could never admit that the tautological character of a proposition might reveal itself by accident, as it were, after we had stumbled upon a proof of it" (p. 319).
29. Although, as Dreben and Floyd (1991, p. 32) point out, Wittgenstein does indeed *originally* believe that his "ab-notation" can be extended to all of logic and appears to arrive at his characterization of logical propositions as tautologies with that in mind. See CL 60–1.
30. Black (1964, p. 319).
31. See again Dreben and Floyd (1991) for an excellent discussion of this whole issue.
32. Bradley (1992, pp. 17–20) goes so far as to attribute this interpretation of "tautology" to Wittgenstein himself.
33. Cf. NB 109: "This is the actual procedure of [the] *old* Logic: it gives

so-called primitive propositions; so-called rules of deduction; and then says that what you get by applying the rules to the propositions is a *logical* proposition that you have *proved*. The truth is, it tells you something about the kind of proposition you have got, viz that it can be derived from the first symbols by these rules of combination (= is a tautology)."

34. Mounce (1981, p. 41) also makes this point.
35. See again Black (1964, p. 338).
36. A number of commentators have wondered at the appearance of the term "symbol" at this point. Thus, for example, Black (1964, p. 338) comments: "In view of what follows immediately, one might have expected to find 'sign' instead." Brockhaus (1991, p. 204) seems to ignore the difference between symbol and sign, even while acknowledging Wittgenstein's intentional use of the former term: "The occurrence of 'symbol' in the first remark and 'sign' in the second [the second sentence of 6.126] – the emphasis, by the way, is Wittgenstein's – implies that insofar as the sense of elementary propositions is guaranteed, we can identify tautologies through purely formal rules for manipulating signs."
37. The possibility of this sort of logical ascent with regard to the variable would appear to have been already introduced at 3.315, where Wittgenstein makes reference to a "nonarbitrarily determined" class of propositions: "If we change a constituent part of a proposition into a variable, there is a class of propositions which are all the values of the resulting variable proposition. This class in general depends on what, by arbitrary agreement, we mean by parts of that proposition. But if we change all those signs, whose meaning was arbitrarily determined, into variables, there always remains such a class. But this is now no longer dependent on any agreement; it depends only on the nature of the proposition. It corresponds to a logical form, to a logical prototype (*einem logischen Urbild*)."
38. See, for example, Cahoone (1995, p. 198).
39. Cf. 6.122 "Whence it follows that we can get on without logical propositions, for we can recognize in an adequate notation the formal properties of the propositions by mere inspection."
40. This point was earlier made on p. 72.
41. See Lewis Carroll (1895). Both Ricketts (1996, p. 216) and Glock (1996, 216) suggest a connection between the Carroll article and the *Tractatus'* view of inference rules.
42. Note that in "Notes Dictated to G. E. Moore in Norway" Wittgenstein in fact immediately follows his account of logical propositions as "forms of proof" with a discussion of the theory of types (NB, p. 109). See also TLP 3.331–3.334 and our discussion on pp. 64–7.
43. In more linguistic terms, this is just to say that the application of the logical constants will never take us beyond the domain of the (significant) proposition.
44. Cf. 5.47:

It is clear that everything which can be said *beforehand* about the form of *all* propositions at all can be said *on one occasion*.
For all logical operations are already contained in the elementary proposition. For "fa" says the same as "(∃x).fx.x = a."
Where there is composition, there is argument and function, and where these are, all logical constants already are.
One could say: the one logical constant is that which all propositions, according to their nature, have in common with one another.
That however is the general form of proposition.

45. I owe this way of putting the matter to Juliet Floyd. Indeed, much of this section has been inspired by her work (unpublished) on the general form of the proposition.
46. See Fogelin (1996, pp. 47–9). Fogelin acknowledges that "it is hard to read this passage without feeling let down," that, indeed, "given the elaborate wind-up, it may even seem a joke" (p. 48). Nonetheless, he maintains that Wittgenstein is "dead serious." Of course, I do not deny that Wittgenstein is here serious – it is a question of what is the import of that seriousness.
47. Cf. also Wittgenstein's claim at the end of the Preface: "And if I am not mistaken in this, then the value of this work secondly consists in the fact that it shows how little has been done when [the problems of philosophy] have been solved" (TLP Preface).
48. One way to understand the middle and later Wittgenstein's shift away from the perspective of the *Tractatus* is to see him as giving up precisely this sharp distinction between general form and logical form, between what can be characterized in advance and what is intrinsic to the particular picture/proposition as such. Wittgenstein's dissatisfaction with the *Tractatus* view expresses itself initially in the so-called Color Exclusion Problem discussed in "Some Remarks on Logical Form," but perhaps more clearly in some of his conversations with Schlick, Waismann, et al. in the late 1920s and early 1930s. Thus, for example, in January 1930, Wittgenstein describes his earlier conception in this way: "I laid down rules for the syntactical use of logical constants, for example 'p.q', and did not think that these rules might have something to do with the inner structure of propositions. What was wrong about my conception was that I believed that the syntax of logical constants could be laid down without paying attention to the inner connection of propositions. That is not how things actually are. I cannot, for example, say that red and blue are at one point simultaneously. Here no logical product can be constructed. Rather, the rules for the logical constants form only a part of a more comprehensive syntax about which I did not yet know anything at that time" (VC 74). Wittgenstein is not, of course, suggesting that in the *Tractatus* he believed that one *could* say that red and blue are at one point simultaneously – this impossibility is explicitly affirmed at 6.3751: "For two colours, e.g. to be at one place in the visual field is impossible,

logically impossible, for it is excluded by the logical structure of colour." Rather, the point is that he had thought this impossibility to be expressible in terms of the logic capturable by his N operator and thus to require the nonelementary nature of propositions ascribing color. In coming to recognize that no analysis of color propositions into logically independent elementary propositions is forthcoming, Wittgenstein is acknowledging the similarity of color exclusion statements (e.g., "Point A is red at time T and point A is blue at time T") *taken as they stand* to nonsensical statements – the pseudo-statements (such as "Socrates is identical") that are, so to speak, incompatible with the logico-pictorial forms. This then brings out the inadequacy, the incorrect multiplicity, of the *Tractatus'* specification of the general propositional form. At the same time, it forces a shift in Wittgenstein's conception of those *unsinnig* pseudo-statements – or, rather, in his conception of how one should *elucidate* their *Unsinnigkeit.* Thus he begins to focus on how the notion of logical inference is applicable in the case of sentences that would seem to share a logical form. As he puts it in his conversations with the Vienna positivists: "At that time [the time of the *Tractatus*] I thought that all inference was based on tautological form. At that time I had not yet seen that an inference can also have the form: This man is 2m tall, therefore he is not 3m tall" (VC 64). For Wittgenstein, this is just to suggest that, in contrast with what the *Tractatus* claims, the inner structure of the proposition, its pictorial character, is describable in terms of rules – that we can to a certain extent offer a grammar of logico-pictorial form. That insight marks the transistion to the far less structured, multifarious approach that characterizes Wittgenstein's work for the rest of his life.

49. The parallels between the *Tractatus* and Kant's *First Critique* have been often noted. See, for example, Pears (1987, especially chapter I), Hacker (1986, pp. 22–3), Brockhaus (1991, especially chapter II), Stenius (1960, pp. 214–18), Glock (1996, p. 200), and Stern (1995, pp. 65–6, 110–13, 132, 147–8).
50. Cf. the opening of the *Notebooks:* "Logic must take care of itself. If syntactical rules for functions can be set up *at all* (*ueberhaupt*), then the whole theory of things, properties, etc. is superfluous. It is also all too obvious that this theory isn't what is in question either in the *Grundgesetze,* or in *Principia Mathematica.* Once more: logic must take care of itself" (NB 2).
51. Frascolla (1994, p. 8) misconstrues 5.25 as suggesting (in part) that "there is no *object* that corresponds to an operation sign as its fixed and distinguishable semantic value." While the *Tractatus* does, of course, deny the existence of logical objects, that is not what is at issue here. After all, to "characterize the sense of a proposition" is not to point to some *thing* – for then propositions would be understood as names.
52. Black (1964, p. 258) disputes Wittgenstein's claim here, since he says that what is said about operations can just as well be said of a function like "x2." Here, however, he is simply ignoring Wittgenstein's special use of the term "function." Even Hylton's much more careful discussion of this

issue in "Functions, Operations, and Sense in Wittgenstein's *Tractatus*" (1997) does not, I suggest, pay sufficient attention to the internal logic of the *Tractatus,* tying Wittgenstein's perspective too closely to that of Frege and Russell.

53. Juliet Floyd (unpublished) has forcefully stressed this point.
54. See also Wittgenstein's reflections in the *Notebooks:* "If a sentence were ever going to be constructable it would already be constructable. We now need a clarification of the concept of the atomic function and the concept 'and so on.' The concept 'and so on' symbolized by ' . . . ' is one of the most important of all and like all the others infinitely fundamental. For it alone justifies us in constructing logic and mathematics 'so on' from the fundamental laws and primitive signs. The 'and so on' makes its appearance right away at the very beginning of the old logic [the logic of Frege and Russell] when it is said that after the primitive signs have been given we can develop one sign after another 'so on.' Without this concept we should be stuck at the primitive signs and could not go *'on'* "(NB 89–90).
55. Note that this occurrence of the ellipsis is *not* an instance of what Wittgenstein is here talking about (in Tractarian terms, it signifies a different symbol). Rather, it constitutes an analogue to a schema for a logical form.
56. In light of this point and what was said just above in note 48 about Wittgenstein's development, one might suppose that his later thought involves showing, in effect, how there *is* an account to be given of why a noise cannot have a weight. But that is not quite accurate; Wittgenstein's later thought is not simply a matter of showing how the Tractarian analysis of the general form of the proposition can be extended to the forms of the elementary propositions. Instead, the rejection of the sharp distinction between general and logico-pictorial form cuts both ways. That is, just as the notion of logical inference is brought to bear in the context of the inner (or, as Wittgenstein might earlier have said, "pictorial") makeup of the proposition, so what we might call the "groundlessness" that characterizes the latter is seen as also applying to the former. Hence, we find the later Wittgenstein in his discussions of rule following fundamentally questioning the "determinacy" that seems to belong to logic.
57. Note here how we are called back to the opening remarks of the *Tractatus* and the association of logic with possibility. As always, Wittgenstein will not *deny* his own seemingly robustly metaphysical claims – he does not assert "p" only later to surreptitiously withdraw it – but, rather, seeks just to make manifest what, in the end, these claims come to.
58. Actually, there is, as Fogelin (1976, pp. 78–82) has pointed out, a difficulty in generating certain multiply quantified formulas – for example, the formula "∀x∃yFxy" – using Wittgenstein's notation, since we are not given any way of making scope distinctions. Fogelin takes this to indicate a "fundamental error" in the logic of the *Tractatus.* It is easy enough, however, to amend the Tractarian notation so as to make it expressively complete, as Geach (1981, pp. 168–71; 1982, pp. 127–8), Soames (1983,

573–89), and Floyd (unpublished) have shown. And since, as Soames also points out, Wittgenstein himself at 4.0411 notes the importance of a notation's ability to express distinctions of scope, it seems overly pedantic to find serious fault with the *Tractatus* for the absence of any explicit instructions on this score.

59. At 5.523, Wittgenstein in fact would appear to suggest that our whole understanding of generality turns around this initial specification: "The generality symbol occurs as an argument" (TLP 5.523). The point, in other words, is that generality is already contained in the "x" in a propositional variable like "x is a table" – the quantifier does not somehow itself manage to confer this property. It is to make this evident that Wittgenstein's notation dispenses altogether with a sign for the quantifier.
60. Mounce (1981, pp. 65–72) argues for this view.
61. See especially *Principia Mathematica,* pp. 38–41.
62. Cf. this *Notebooks* assertion from 1915: "All APPEARS to be nearer the content of the proposition than to the form. . . . Generality is essentially connected with the elementary FORM. The liberating word – ?" (NB 39; caps Wittgenstein's).
63. It is important for our understanding of Wittgenstein's development to here reiterate the point made last chapter (see note 17, chapter II) about how he comes to see himself as confused on this issue. For while the *Tractatus'* emphasis on the ellipsis is meant to bring out the unclarity of the notion of an infinite disjunction, the idea of a complete analysis seems ultimately to rest on this conception. After all, the possibility of *completing* the analysis of this occurrence of "on the table" can only be realized if, in the end, we *can* make a comprehensive list of spatial locations. In the *Tractatus,* then, the dots in the above formal series must be understood as marking only some sort of present limitation on our analytical capacities, whereas the later Wittgenstein brings out much more sharply how, for him, it makes *no sense* to imagine such a possibility.
64. Or more properly, "schema for a variable," since ξ serves only as a placeholder for some particular propositional variable.
65. Note how the use of the term *vertreten* here mirrors its use at 2.31 and 3.22, where, we recall, it served to describe how the pictorial/propositional constituents "stand in" (or "go proxy") for their counterparts in the world.
66. Here I am again indebted to Juliet Floyd (unpublished), who develops this idea in an original and very illuminating discussion of the *Tractatus'* treatment of "number."
67. Cf. Wittgenstein's 1919 letter to Russell: "I suppose you didn't understand the way, how I separate in the old notation of generality what is in it truth-function and what is purely generality. A general prop[osition] is A truth-function of *all* PROP[OSITION]S of a certain form" (NB 131); caps Wittgenstein's).
68. Wittgenstein also acknowledges this in the same 1919 letter to Russell

referred to in the previous note: "You are quite right in saying 'N($\bar{\xi}$)' may also be made to mean ~p v ~q v ~r v. . . . But this doesn't matter!" (NB 131).

69. See Fogelin (1976, p. 80): "The expression "(x:N(fx))" [Geach's way of expressing one application of N to a function "fx"] specifies (or is shorthand for) a set of propositions that is the result of possibly infinitely many (unordered) applications of the operator N to a possibly infinite set of propositions." Fogelin then goes on to argue that this requirement is inconsistent with 5.32's assertion that all such applications must be finite. As he puts it: "If the set of base propositions is infinite, then nothing will count as the immediate predecessor of the final application of the operation N in the construction of a universally quantified proposition" (p. 81).

Chapter IV

1. For accuracy, we would have to add here "in a certain respect." For the fundamental distinction we have emphasized between *the* general form of the proposition and the (anumerical) logical forms entails that no systematic presentation can be given of the *inner* structure of the proposition, its internal relation to the world.
2. Besides, Wittgenstein's later thought is not in a fundamentally different position with respect to the particular problem we are here addressing: we still may wonder about how that work is to be applied to philosophical confusions that it does not specifically treat.
3. Cf. PO 165: "Indeed we can only convict someone else of a mistake if he acknowledges that this really is the expression of his feeling. For only if he acknowledges it as such, is it the correct expression. (Psychoanalysis). What the other person acknowledges is the analogy I am proposing to him as the source of his thought."
4. Cf. CV 16: "Working in philosophy – like work in architecture in many respects – is really more a working on oneself. On one's own interpretation. On one's way of seeing things. (And what one expects of them)."
5. Conant (1998; pp. 247–8) makes a similar point.
6. In a similar vein, Rhees (1998, p. 40) asserts: "And that is what has to be pressed against those who think of philosophy as therapeutic. Something we have to indulge in because some people are unfortunate. You could never understand why Wittgenstein (and others) have wanted to compare philosophy with poems, in that case. The man who finds life difficult. And the man who wants to 'put the difficulties right'."
7. One cannot but think here of Russell's ongoing worry about the need for immediate contact between the mind and reality, as it is expressed in his early rejection of idealism, in his notion of knowledge by acquaintance, and so forth. For Wittgenstein, Russell's attempts to "secure" this connection through some kind of elaborate account are paradigmatic of

philosophical confusion. We might say that the essential thrust of the *Tractatus* is to get us to see that such a connection can only be shown.

8. Note that the identical phrase appears at 6.52 of the *Tractatus,* although in an apparently different context (see the following footnote). Note also that in both the *Tractatus* and the *Notebooks* the quoted phrase is prefaced by the words "We *feel* that"; Wittgenstein is describing the *sense* that gives rise to philosophical perplexity, but at the same time emphasizing that it is no *more* than a sense, a feeling.
9. It should be noted that this *Notebooks* passage occurs in the context of Wittgenstein's discussion of what he calls "the urge towards the mystical." Given the standard interpretation of the Tractarian notion of showing as resting on the possibility of an ineffable content, the tendency amongst commentators (Russell included) has been to understand the early Wittgenstein as in fact endorsing some version of mysticism. On this reading, it would then be mistaken to substitute, as I do, "philosophy" (which Wittgenstein is seen as wanting in some sense to counter) for "the mystical" in that passage. But I would urge that Wittgenstein's attitude toward mysticism is not univocal, that he cannot simply be described in general as "pro" or "con." For if we look at the whole of the remark from *Notebooks* 51, it seems quite clear that in this context anyway he is decidedly *not* embracing a mystical stance, at least in the sense of imagining an ineffable "answer" to all outstanding nonscientific questions. The response he ultimately points to does not lie in a wordless flood of insight, but just in the recognition that "there are no questions any more." That familiar-sounding "solution" would suggest that the mystical urge is seen as here appearing in very philosophical guise. By contrast, however, I believe that we misconstrue the *Tractatus'* overall aims when we see Wittgenstein, as Conant (see especially 1991) and Diamond sometimes imply, as fundamentally *rejecting* any notion of mysticism. While it may certainly be granted that the text's notion of showing does not involve a gesture toward an ineffable truth (and that one way of understanding the mystic would be to attribute to him the desire to make such a gesture), the reader is not thereby committed to attributing to Wittgenstein the view that "everything" must be stateable (whatever that would mean) – still less to supposing that the notion of an ineffable content is Wittgenstein's real *target* in the *Tractatus.*
10. Shields (1993, p. 63) makes a similar observation: "[Wittgenstein] seems to have more respect for someone who is seriously enmeshed and bothered by metaphysical difficulties, than for those who were never bothered at all. One gets the impression that it is somehow better to undergo a prolonged spiritual struggle in the pursuit of righteousness, than to follow Aristotle's ideal and to do good spontaneously out of habit."
11. Recall Wittgenstein's claim in the Preface: "The book will, therefore, draw a limit to thinking, or rather – not to thinking, but to the expression of thoughts; for, in order to draw a limit to thinking we should have to be able to think both sides of this limit (we should therefore have to be able

to think what cannot be thought). The limit can, therefore, only be drawn in language and what lies on the other side of the limit will be simply nonsense" (TLP p. 27). Cf. also this remark from the "Big Typescript": "As I have often said, philosophy does not lead me to any renunciation, since I do not abstain from saying something, but rather abandon a certain combination of words as senseless. In another sense, however, philosophy requires a resignation, but one of feeling and not of intellect. And maybe that is what makes it so difficult for many. It can be difficult not to use an expression, just as it is difficult to hold back tears, or an outburst of anger" (PO 161).

12. One is also reminded here of this remark from *Culture and Value:* "If anyone should think he has solved the problem of life and feel like telling himself that everything is quite easy now, he can see that he is wrong just by recalling that there was a time when this 'solution' had not been discovered; but it must have been possible to live *then* too and the solution which has now been discovered seems fortuitous in relation to how things were then. And it is the same in the study of logic. If there were a 'solution' to the problems of logic (philosophy) we should only need to caution ourselves that there was a time when they had not been solved (and even at that time people must have known how to live and think)" (CV 4).
13. In this vein, it is sometimes suggested that Wittgenstein's aim is therefore to return us to "the ordinary"; see, e.g., Putnam's (1993, pp. vii ff.) account of what he calls the " 'end of philosophy' reading of Wittgenstein". But this is misleading. It implies that there is some special state or experience that philosophers are somehow blinded to. This, for Wittgenstein, is nonsense. To posit a general notion of "ordinary experience" is to engage in just the sort of *a priori* categorization that the *Tractatus,* as we have seen, seeks to explode. Despite the philosopher's yearning to see his enterprise – even in its disappearance – as aiming toward some definite end, Wittgenstein will not allow us to say that he is returning us *to* anything in particular. There is simply the process of being freed from philosophical illusions.
14. One might then say that, in a certain sense, for Wittgenstein only *I* can recognize my propositions as nonsense. That, of course, is not to deny that another might point out to me the apparent *peculiarity* of my utterances, but I alone can call them *nonsense.* The possibility of expressing matters in this way can help us to see the importance of solipsism for Wittgenstein, why this notion is particularly prominent in the closing pages of the book (see especially TLP 5.62–5.641). Compare this also with the similar idea that we saw expressed in connection with the discussion of analysis, the claim that "I know what I mean" by the vague proposition (see NB 70 and pp. 212 ff. of this study).
15. Cf. this emphatic declaration at the beginning of section 86 of the "Big Typescript": "DIFFICULTY OF PHILOSOPHY NOT THE INTELLECTUAL DIFFICULTY OF THE SCIENCES, BUT THE DIFFICULTY OF A CHANGE

OF ATTITUDE. RESISTANCES OF THE WILL (*des willens*) MUST BE OVERCOME" (PO 161; caps Wittgenstein's).

16. Or one could say, in the language of 6.373, that it is a reluctance to acknowledge the world as *independent* of my will.
17. By contrast, the state to which the *Tractatus* aims to bring us – what Wittgenstein at 6.43 calls the "world of the happy" – is characterized just by complete agreement between the self and its world. Thus, the *Notebooks* remarks: "The happy life seems to be in some sense more *harmonious* than the unhappy" (NB 78). Of course, for Wittgenstein such harmony is not a genuine *property* of an individual's life, one element that might be present or absent, but rather an internal feature of his way of relating to the world. For this reason then the *Tractatus* speaks of the ethical world as "wax[ing] and wan[ing] as a whole" (TLP 6.43).
18. Still, we note that in PI 133 the original demand for "complete clarity" and the complete disappearance of philosophical problems remains.

BIBLIOGRAPHY

Abbreviations used:

BEG *Begriffsschrift*
BLA *Basic Laws of Arithmetic*
CL *Wittgenstein's Lectures, Cambridge, 1930–32*
CP *Frege's Collected Papers on Mathematics, Logic, and Philosophy*
CV *Culture and Value*
D *Denkbewegungen: Tagebucher 1930–1932, 1936–1937*
FA *Foundations of Arithmetic*
LF "Letters to Ludwig von Ficker"
NB *Notebooks 1914–16*
PG *Philosophical Grammar*
PI *Philosophical Investigations*
PO *Philosophical Occasions*
PR *Philosophical Remarks*
PT *Prototractatus*
PW *Translations from the Philosophical Writings of Gottlob Frege*
TLP *Tractatus Logico-Philosophicus*
VC *Ludwig Wittgenstein and the Vienna Circle*
Z *Zettel*

Allaire, E. B., 1966. "The *Tractatus:* Nominalistic or Realistic?," in *Essays on Wittgenstein's* Tractatus, I. M. Copi and R. W. Beard (eds.). New York: Macmillan.

Anscombe, G. E., 1959. *An Introduction to Wittgenstein's Tractatus.* New York: Harper & Row.

Biletzki, A., in press. *(Over)Interpreting Wittgenstein.* Berkeley and Los Angeles: University of California Press.

Black, M., 1964. *A Companion to Wittgenstein's Tractatus.* Ithaca, NY: Cornell University Press.

Bradley, R., 1992. *The Nature of All Being: A Study of Wittgenstein's Modal Atomism.* New York: Oxford University Press.

Brockhaus, R., 1991. *Pulling Up the Ladder.* LaSalle, WI: Open Court.

Cahoone L., 1995. *The Ends of Philosophy.* Albany: State University of New York Press.

Carnap, R., 1937. *The Logical Syntax of Language.* London: Routledge & Kegan Paul.

———, 1979. *Philosophy and Logical Syntax.* New York: AMS Press.

Carrol, L., 1895. "What the Tortoise Said to Achilles," *Mind* n.s., IV.

Cavell, S., 1979. *The Claim of Reason.* New York: Oxford University Press.

Cerbone, D., 2000. "How to Do Things With Wood: Wittgenstein, Frege, and the Problem of Illogical Thought," in *The New Wittgenstein,* A. Crary and R. Read (eds.), pp. 292–314. London: Routledge.

Conant, J., 1989. "Must We Show What We Cannot Say," in *The Senses of Stanley Cavell,* R. Fleming and M. Payne (eds.), pp. 242–83. Lewisburg, PA: Bucknell University Press.

———, 1991. "Throwing Away the Top of the Ladder." *Yale Review,* vol. 79, pp. 328–64.

———, 1993. "Kierkegaard, Wittgenstein, and Nonsense," in *Pursuits of Reason,* T. Cohen, P. Guyer, and H. Putnam (eds.), pp. 195–224. Lubbock: Texas Tech University Press.

———, 1998. "Wittgenstein on Meaning and Use." *Philosophical Investigations,* vol. 21, pp. 222–50.

———, 2000. "Elucidation and Nonsense in Frege and the Early Wittgenstein," in *The New Wittgenstein,* A. Crary and R. Read (eds.), pp. 174–217. London: Routledge.

Copi, I. M., 1966. "Objects, Properties, and Relations in the *Tractatus,*" in *Essays on Wittgenstein's Tractatus,* I. M. Copi and R. W. Beard (eds.). New York: Macmillan.

Diamond, C., 1991. *The Realistic Spirit.* Cambridge, MA: MIT Press.

———, 2000. "Ethics, Imagination, and the Method of Wittgenstein's *Tractatus,*" in *The New Wittgenstein,* A. Crary and R. Read (eds.), pp. 149–73. London: Routledge.

Dreben, B. Lectures, 1991–98; unpublished lecture transcriptions, 1962–98.

Dreben, B. and Floyd, J., 1991. "Tautology: How Not to Use a Word." *Synthese 87,* pp. 23–49.

Dummett, M., 1991. *The Logical Basis of Metaphysics.* Cambridge, MA: Harvard University Press.

Evans, E., 1966. "*Tractatus* 3.1432," in *Essays on Wittgenstein's Tractatus,* I. M. Copi and R. W. Beard (eds.), pp. 133–5. New York: Macmillan.

Floyd, J., 1997. Unpublished lecture.

———, 1998. "The Uncaptive Eye: Solipsism in Wittgenstein's *Tractatus,*" in *Loneliness,* L. Rouner (ed.), pp. 79–108. Notre Dame, IN: University of Notre Dame Press.

———, in press. "Number and Ascriptions of Number in Wittgenstein's *Trac-*

tatus," in *From Frege to Wittgenstein: Perspectives on Early Analytic Philosophy,* E. Rech (ed.). New York: Oxford University Press.
Fogelin, R., 1976. *Wittgenstein.* London: Routledge & Kegan Paul.
———, 1996 (2nd ed.). *Wittgenstein.* London: Routledge & Kegan Paul.
Frascolla, P., 1994. *Wittgenstein's Philosophy of Mathematics.* London: Routledge.
Frege, G., 1964. *Basic Laws of Arithmetic.* M. Furth (ed.), M. Furth (trans.). Berkeley and Los Angeles: University of California Press.
———, 1967. *Begriffsschrift, A Formula Language, Modeled Upon That of Arithmetic, For Pure Thought,* in *From Frege to Godel: A Source Book in Mathematical Logic, 1879–1931,* J. van Heijenoort (ed.). Cambridge, MA: Harvard University Press.
———, 1980 (3rd ed.). *Translations from the Philosophical Writings of Gottob Frege,* M. Black and P. Geach (trans.). Oxford: Basil Blackwell.
———, 1980. *The Foundations of Arithmetic,* J. L. Austin (trans.). Oxford: Basil Blackwell.
———, 1984. *Collected Papers on Mathematics, Logic, and Philosophy.* B. McGuinness (ed.), M. Black, et. al. (trans.). Oxford: Basil Blackwell.
Friedlander, E., 1992. "Expressions of Judgment," Ph.D. Dissertation. Harvard University.
Geach, P. T., 1976. "Saying and Showing in Frege and Wittgenstein," in *Essays on Wittgenstein in Honour of G. H. von Wright,* J. Hintikka (ed.), *Acta Philosophica Fennica* 28. Amsterdam: North-Holland Pub. Co.
———, 1981. "Wittgenstein's Operator N." *Analysis* 41, no. 4, pp. 168–71.
Glock, H., 1996. "Necessity and Normativity," in *The Cambridge Companion to Wittgenstein,* H. Sluga and D. Stern (eds.), pp. 198–225. Cambridge: Cambridge University Press.
Goldfarb, W., 1997. "Metaphysics and Nonsense: On Cora Diamond's *The Realistic Spirit." Journal of Philosophical Research* 22, pp. 57–72.
———, unpublished. "Objects, Names, and Realism in the *Tractatus."*
Grasshof, G., 1997. "Hertzian Objects in Wittgenstein's *Tractatus." British Journal of the History of Philosophy* 5(1), pp. 87–119.
Hacker, P. M. S., 1972. *Insight and Illusion: Themes in the Philosophy of Wittgenstein.* New York: Oxford University Press.
———, 1986 (revised 2nd ed.). *Insight and Illusion: Themes in the Philosophy of Wittgenstein.* New York: Oxford University Press.
———, 2000. "Was He Trying to Whistle It?," in *The New Wittgenstein,* A. Crary and R. Read (eds.), pp. 353–87. London: Routledge.
Hallet, G., 1977. *A Companion to Wittgenstein's "Philosophical Investigations."* Ithaca, NY: Cornell University Press.
Hintikka, M. and Hintikka, J., 1986. *Investigating Wittgenstein.* Oxford: Blackwell.
Hylton, P., 1997. "Functions, Operations, and Sense in Wittgenstein's *Tractatus,"* in *Early Analytic Philosophy,* W. W. Tait (ed.), pp. 91–106. La Salle, WI: Open Court.
Kant, I., 1929. *Critique of Pure Reason.* N. K. Smith (trans.). London: Macmillan.

Kremer, M., 1997. "Contextualism and Holism in the Early Wittgenstein: From *Prototractatus* to *Tractatus*." *Philosophical Topics*, vol. 25, pp. 87–120.

McDonough, R., 1986. *The Argument of the Tractatus: Its Relevance to Contemporary Theories of Logic, Language, Mind, and Philosophical Truth*. Buffalo: State University of New York Press.

McGinn, M., 1999. "Between Metaphysics and Nonsense: Elucidation in Wittgenstein's *Tractatus*." *The Philosophical Quarterly*, vol. 49, pp. 491–513.

Moore, G. E., 1901–5. "Nativism and Empiricism," in *Dictionary of Philosophy and Psychology*, Baldwin, J. (ed.), vol. 2, pp. 129–32. New York: Macmillan.

Mounce, H. O., 1981. *Wittgenstein's Tractatus: An Introduction*. Chicago: University of Chicago Press.

Pears, D., 1987. *The False Prison: A Study of the Development of Wittgenstein's Philosophy* (2 vols.). Oxford: Clarendon Press.

———, unpublished. Paper delivered at the 1998 meeting of the Boston Colloquium for Philosophy of Science.

Pitcher, G., 1964. *The Philosophy of Wittgenstein*. Englewood Cliffs, NJ: Prentice Hall.

Putnam, H., 1993. "Preface: Introducing Cavell," in *Pursuits of Reason*, T. Cohen, P. Guyer, and H. Putnam (eds.), pp. vii–xii. Lubbock: Texas Tech University Press.

———, 1998. "Floyd, Wittgenstein, and Loneliness," in "The Uncaptive Eye: Solipsism in Wittgenstein's *Tractatus*," in *Loneliness*, L. Rouner (ed.), pp. 109–14. Notre Dame, IN: University of Notre Dame Press.

Ramsey, F., 1931. *The Foundations of Mathematics and Other Logical Essays*. London: Routledge.

Reid, L., 1998. "Wittgenstein's Ladder: The *Tractatus* and Nonsense." *Philosophical Investigations*, vol. 21, pp. 97–151.

Rhees, R., 1997. *Rush Rhees on Religion and Philosophy*. D. Z. Philips (ed.). Cambridge: Cambridge University Press.

———, 1998. *Wittgenstein and the Possibility of Discourse*. D. Z. Philips (ed.). Cambridge: Cambridge University Press.

Ricketts, T., 1986. "Objectivity of Objecthood: Frege's Metaphysics of Judgment," in *Frege Synthesized*, L. Haaparanta and J. Hintikka (eds.). Dordrecht: Kluwer Academic Publishers.

———, 1996. "Pictures, Logic, and the Limits of Sense in Wittgenstein's *Tractatus*," in *The Cambridge Companion to Wittgenstein*, H. Sluga and D. G. Stern (eds.), pp. 59–99. Cambridge: Cambridge University Press.

Russell, B., 1938 (2nd ed.). *Principles of Mathematics*. New York: W. W. Norton.

———, 1984. *Theory of Knowledge The 1913 Manuscript*. London: G. Allen & Unwin.

———, 1985. *The Philosophy of Logical Atomism*. LaSalle, WI: Open Court.

Schwyzer, H. R. G., 1966. "Wittgenstein's Picture Theory of Language," in *Essays on Wittgenstein's Tractatus*, I. M. Copi and R. W. Beard (eds.), pp. 271–88. New York: Macmillan.

Sellars, W., 1966. "Naming and Saying," in *Essays on Wittgenstein's Tractatus*, I. Copi and R. W. Beard (eds.), pp. 249–70. New York: Macmillan.

Shields, P. R., 1993. *Logic and Sin in the Writings of Ludwig Wittgenstein.* Chicago: University of Chicago Press.

Soames, S., 1983. "Generality, Truth Functions, and Expressive Capacity in the *Tractatus." Philosophical Review,* XCII, No. 4, pp. 573–89.

Stenius, E., 1960. *Wittgenstein's Tractatus.* Ithaca, NY: Cornell University Press.

Stern, D. G., 1995. *Wittgenstein on Mind and Language.* New York: Oxford University Press.

Stripling S., 1978. "The Picture Theory of Meaning: An Interpretation of Wittgenstein's *Tractatus Logico-Philosophicus,*" Ph.D. Dissertation. Pennsylvania State University.

Weinberg, J., 1966. "Are There Ultimate Simples?," in *Essays on Wittgenstein's Tractatus,* I. Copi and R. W. Beard (eds.), pp. 75–85. New York: Macmillan.

Weiner, J., 1990. *Frege in Perspective.* Ithaca, NY: Cornell University Press.

Whitehead A. N., 1978. *Process and Reality: An Essay in Cosmology.* New York: Free Press.

Williams, B., 1974. "Wittgenstein and Idealism," in *Understanding Wittgenstein,* G. Versey (ed.), pp. 76–95. Ithaca, NY: Cornell University Press.

Winch, P., 1992. "Persuasion," in *Midwest Studies in Philosophy,* vol. 16, *The Wittgenstein Legacy,* P. A. French, T. E. Uehling, and H. K. Wettstein (eds.), pp. 123–37. Notre Dame, IN: University of Notre Dame Press.

Witherspoon, E., 2000. "Conceptions of Nonsense in Carnap and Wittgenstein," in *The New Wittgenstein,* A. Crary and R. Read (eds.), pp. 315–49. London: Routledge.

Wittgenstein, L., 1922. *Tractatus Logico-Philosophicus.* C. K. Ogden (trans.). London: Routledge & Kegan Paul.

———, 1958 (2nd ed.). *Philosophical Investigations.* G. E. M. Anscombe and R. Rhees (eds.), G. E. M. Anscombe (trans.), second edition. Oxford: Basil Blackwell.

———, 1967. *Zettel.* G. E. M. Anscombe and G. H. von Wright (eds.), G. E. M. Anscombe (trans.). Berkeley and Los Angeles: University of California Press.

———, 1971. *Prototractatus – An Early Version of Tractatus Logico-Philosophicus.* B. F. McGuiness, T. Nyberg, and G. H. von Wright (eds.), D. F. Pears and B. F. McGuiness (trans.). Ithaca, NY: Cornell University Press.

———, 1974. *Philosophical Grammar.* R. Rhees (ed.), A. Kenny (trans.). Berkeley and Los Angeles: University of California Press.

———, 1975. *Philosophical Remarks.* R. Rhees (ed.), R. Hargreaves and R. White (trans.). Chicago: University of Chicago Press.

———, 1979. "Letters to Ludwig von Ficker," in *Wittgenstein: Sources and Perspectives,* C. G. Luckhardt (ed.). Ithaca, NY: Cornell University Press.

———, 1979. *Ludwig Wittgenstein and the Vienna Circle: Conversations Recorded by Friedrich Waismann.* B. McGuinness (ed.), J. Schulte and B. McGuiness (trans.). Oxford: Blackwell.

———, 1979 (2nd ed.). *Notebooks 1914–16.* G. H. von Wright and G. E. M. Anscombe (eds.), G. E. M. Anscombe (trans.). Chicago: University of Chicago Press.

———, 1980 (2nd ed.). *Culture and Value.* G. H. Von Wright (ed.), P. Winch (trans.). Chicago: University of Chicago Press.

———, 1980. *Wittgenstein's Lectures, Cambridge, 1930–32.* D. Lee (ed.). Oxford: Basil Blackwell.

———, 1993. *Philosophical Occasions.* J. C. Klagge and A. Nordmann (eds.). Indianapolis, IN: Hackett.

———, 1997. *Denkbewegungen: Tagebucher 1930–32, 1936–37.* I. Somavilla (ed.). Innsbruck: Haymon-Verlag.

INDEX